All icons appearing in this book are derived from
SURVIVAL ON LAND AND SEA; SURVIVAL
– Jungle / Desert / Arctic / Ocean;
and SURVIVAL FM 21-76;
all prepared for the United States Army, Navy,
and Air Forces between 1941-1957.

THE ACCOMPLICES:
A Writ Large Press Book

theaccomplices.org

THE ACCOMPLICES

Navigating With(out) Instruments

poetry—micro essays—notes to self

traci kato-kiriyama

Dedicated to
The Continuum –
all the bridge builders, fire starters,
subtle markers, direct talkers, humble sages,
teachers, nurses, healers, counselors, therapists,
misfit and alien beings,
big sistahs, siblings, cousins, mentors,
the ghosts, the bones,
and impossible survivors
who raised and raise me.
We are here.
I
(want to)
stay alive
because of you.

For Ma.
For the rjf.

CONTENTS

warning
a book
of
poetry
is
a
trigger
warning
a
book
of
poetry
is
a
trigger
warning
a
book
of
poetry
is
a
trigger
warning
a
book
of
poetry
is
a
trigger
warning
a book
of
poetry
is
a
trigger
warning
a
book
of
poetry
is
a
trigger

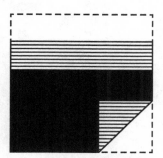

**Have Abandoned Plane,
Walking in this
Direction** ➡

remember, all the children whom were never born to me

the   little   raspy   voice   one

who can name all the presidents

the   big haired   one

with a   smile   that screams for

revolution

and popsicles

the   squeaky   retort   and   gentle   foot   one

i saw while sitting there at the beach

every   little   one

I see while sitting anywhere

at every awful beach

versions
        of a   future

           a given

               back in my twenties

all the while   i said my window was closing
              but i still   knew   i

had   time

this was supposed to happen,   after

              all

       all   or   any

         of   them

especially the   ones
        who came to me in my dreams:

the curly haired cutie pie who rounded the corner

off the hallway   to up and   fly   into

my

arms

i   still   catch him   sometimes

while standing

here

frozen

in my kitchen

or

the   goofball

who   tapped   me   on   the forehead

too   early

in the morning

begging   for   waffles

and presents

i   still   see them   even after the

decorations are   taken

                              down

(they)   construct the   perfect

                    imperfect

                                                  child

some tiny   one   i
                                        imagined

would be   both   of my body
                           and
                           dropped off at my door
                                    at their age of 2

                         ready to go
                         ready to walk
                         ready to use
                         the toilet on their

own
(my fantasies don't need to struggle)

that   little   one   who would   frustrate me send me to
fits challenge   me   to

the point of
knowing:

i was gettin' mine

the   growing
one

who would be

aging
alongside

me

feels

like   they should   be

(would've been)

here

by

now

(re)dream: curly haired cutie pie

He was a little he
big curly hair
mixed blood of my blood
or not

Maybe four or five when
he sped down the hall
around the corner of the kitchen
open arms toward me
running jump to fly into
a future memory passed right
by me

That is all i know
or is it
all i can remember
but he was mine as much as
any little one could be

Maybe there is more to recall:
he had a big laugh like mine
and a grand smile
as he grew older and older
he became queerer and queerer
bigger and tougher
and he determined to keep his smile
and we never warred
and we always debated
and we spent less time together
and we loved each other

like i could never love
any other
or is that just what is said
happens
when a child enters into your life
to blossom your adulthood, of
course, well, of course

And one day
he went to a grave
and placed a single cymbidium
on a patch of land
no one else was left to care to visit

He planted a joke
into the earth underneath his knees
and swore to the birch tree above his head
that the grounds of the cemetery
shook because of
the chattering set of teeth
buried below

That is my mother, cracking up,
he said
i swear i can hear her laugh
penetrate the wind

Then he
rose to his feet and
left me alone again

Sperm bank: the problem with height

Wanted: donor of Okinawan descent
Reason 1: honor rj's mom who is full Uchinanchu
Reason 2: high rate of centenarian in the Ryukyu Kingdom

Sperm bank of reputable nature and sizable expense:

No donor allowed under 5'9"

N.T.S.
No wonder.
No Okinawa-raised sperm in sight.

My Periodic Wavering On Pregnancy, circa my 30-something years:

stop sending paper infants to my doorbell

or when the babies come scratching
outside my front door
i will say i'm sorry
but i'm out of milk to share

cease your tapping
we're a home full of cats
and possums and raccoons
the rest of wild kingdom
out back
will tell you
we're maxed out here

please go away
and take these Parent magazines
with you
                    (who subscribed me to this list?)

I'm clearly on the late-30-something roster
overseen by the
Geriatric Ovary Jury
clocking us
over the emergency boards,
red lights flashing and
sirens screaming
next to our names

I am number 73
and they are after me,
hard

They send mailers on IVF
sperm banks
doulas
and DIY turkey baster methods
pushing my buttons,
reminding me of too many a friend
who said
"C'mon, you have to, there are
too many assholes having babies...
don't let the assholes be the only
ones to have babies."

all these calls to action
must suggest
I have some time
but it is running
running out fast

and
there it is again

another baby
knocking
at my door

N.T.S.

DNA studies purport that memory is passed on through offspring.
Quantum physics theorists, sociologists, and psychologists consider consciousness and its relation to inter-generational existence.
We are thus co-creating pan-generational consciousness through the past, present and future in concert with each other
       Can any of this be passed on *outside* of the vessel of DNA?
Will my consciousness contribute to the greater collective beyond my time here...if I don't express it?

N.T.S.
N.T.W.

One conclusion = while occupying space on this plane(t), people specifically without children need to write out and share their contributions to the greater physical world beyond the vibrations of our daily existence, if we are to be a positive factor in the evolution of our collective epigenetics.
One's consciousness can impact and thus seep into an Other's bones.
If nothing else, this is...this must be...some type of PERMISSION to write down, write out, create, and communicate our dreams, visions, philosophies, and practices in life. We are after all, here...birthing.

N.T.C.

Please do not assume so much of the person walking
this earth at this time without child – That there has been
a simple path of deciding against adopting or bearing child,
even when you meet them at the moment of being at peace
with not adopting or bearing child.
That there hasn't been loss, contemplation,
depletion, letting go, debate, fighting with self or partner.
That there has only been loss, depletion, fighting with self
or partner. That there hasn't been the extreme depths of
unbelievable love, joy, passion, peace, exploration, creation.
That there hasn't been birthing.

Instead, invite us in. We can be Revolutionary Aunties &
Radical Siblings.
And you could probably use the support

N.T.R.

Write a letter to your future great, great grandchild,
whether real or imaginary, whether you ever wanted a child
or not.
The letter must include three questions to yourself, then
to the child.
Mail it to someone
you trust. Or read it aloud once, then bury it.

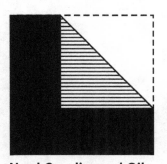

**Need Gasoline and Oil
Plane is Flyable**

Death Moment – 42

Bury the last question of every month and every missed
period and every flu and cold and odd bump and lump

Bury the morbid lists and letters and hypotheticals that
drive rj crazy

Bury that moment we looked at each other from across the
room, cursing not the disease or the diagnosis but each
others inconvenient plans for the next week

Bury each fear with each death of those who go before their
time. Bury the lost time. Bury no curiosity but the one of
How much time left. Bury the clocks all of them.

Somewhere Between Orlando and a Biopsy

*(after the victims and survivors of the June 12, 2016
tragedy at the Pulse nightclub in Orlando)*

my left breast
goes into a hole
center, of a long table

i think
that is odd
why is the hole in the center

i lay down on my stomach
to position myself
at the table's midsection

the vice
comes in and
the nurse's hand

tugs and pulls
and we converse
any way

there is a doctor
coming soon named
needle

hello
needle, hurry up
i will say

the nurse
will pat my back
at its center

and ask me what
I do
for a living

this is always
the tricky part between strangers
keep it light or keep it real?

tell her everything?
cut to the chase?
what do i have to lose?

we will
be there
for forty minutes

she will have
my left breast in her right hand
for most of it

enough time for honesty
and judgment without
the sting of attachment

if what i say
centers around
her discomfort

then she will still have my
left breast in a vice
and we will be even

i tell her everything
i cut to the chase
i have nothing to lose

i speak
in lean terms,
i center on my truths

me, as queer,
me, with mind split between
yesterday's shooting and tonight's vigil

me, in vigilance for the dead as much as
for those left running for cover
in the days, weeks, and years of backlash

me, in love and solidarity with my
family of queer folk, Muslim community,
our immigrant families and

the list continues
my politics are not shy, my words attempt
to carve an avenue on this cold biopsy table

she looks me in the eye, she listens
and nods
a map emerges between us

she says
she wishes
she could join me

there is work and life and no time
and she tells me
"you go to this vigil for me, too"

i wish i could nod back
but i can't move
from the center

instead, i moan
she understands that
language much better than i do

she speaks in possibility
and kindness and
grabs my hand

within minutes
i chart her origins, we locate an
old dream of her, once a painter

within minutes, she
navigates my politics
and my relations

she nods
as i moan
and squeeze her fingers

my half-numb breast
is stuck in a
vice with a needle

at its center
and all is good
and i am fine

Week of Diagnosis – day 1 –
The Things A Doctor Should Never Say

A doctor really shouldn't do what she did.

A doctor should enter the room calmly. A doctor should stay in the room once she's opened my file instead of rushing in and out.

A doctor should look like she knows what she's doing, if only for the sake of the patient and the patient's partner who is now frozen in place because the doctor can't just say the word.

A doctor should not begin by saying:
This is so hard. I don't know how to say this. You're so young.

A doctor should begin with:

I don't want you to worry. You will be fine. There is amazing technology now and we will fight this so hard, it never comes back.

I take joycey's hand and tell her not to worry.

I look my doctor in the eye and say, *It's okay...just say it.*

If anything, a doctor should just say it.

Because I can't.

Not yet.

The doctor must go first.

Week after Diagnosis – day 9

prayer appears   *Calcification:*

                                            happens with build

                                            up

                 a mass is observed   *in body   tissue, blood,*

                                            vessels, or organs.

the other way around   *This build up can*

                                            harden and disrupt

the agnostic accepts prayer   *body's normal process*

                 prayer loves fragility
                 cancer swallows vanity

                 on the tongue: desert

                                            horizon

                                            need

List of Fears	List of Needs/(Re)plies to
Diagnosis	

(re)search / secret(e)s

[i know
you (mean)(need
me) (to
be) well]

CAUSES OF
COGNITIVE
PROBLEMS

cancer survivors   "just stay strong"
commonly
use the term
chemobrain to
describe problems
with thinking   "don't cry"
clearly after
treatment with.
Chemotherapy

(silence) on other end of call

behavioral and
emotional
changes. This   =
includes
irrational
behavior   end of negotiation on
potential (gig)

Mood swings   "you
Intense anger or   have
Crying or   to stay
Socially unsuitable behavior   positive"

the level of these symptoms often de(e)p-
End on several factors:
- *a person's age*   "you
- *STRESS level*   know
- *history of de(e)pression and anxiety*   you
- *coping skills*   can
- *access to psychological resources*   beat
- *types of treatment*   this"

N.T.S.
what is going on.
I can't keep track of
how many times a
person has now shared
with me about their
illness and how they
are keeping it a
secret.
and every single one was
Asian –
and of all the others
who've shared with me
their book, their t-shirts
or totes announcing their
cancer, 9 out of 10 were not.
Just remember the person
who freaked out on you
and quit negotiating that gig.
Don't assume anything –
the stigma is still very real.

side(affects)effects
[of medication]   in p(re)sent time

confusion	*we don't know*	
calf pain	*if taking*	1) "Is it gone?"
/ swelling	*reduces*	
unusual	*number*	
changes	*of cancers*	2) "Are you in remission?"
in your	*lifetime*	
monthly	*if only*	
period	*delays*	3) "Are you feeling better?"
amount	*cancers*	
or	*if taking*	
timing	*taking*	4) "Are you cancer-free?"
of	*helps*	
bleeding	*a*	
pain or pressure	*woman*	5) "I'm glad you're okay."
below	*live*	
your belly	*longer*	
numb	*we don't*	6) "You're done with all
tingling		your
skin	*know*	treatments,
condition		right?"

1) even ghosts leave shadows.
2) last elevator to my right.
3) Vitamin D.
4) Contemplate 102-year plan.
5) _____.
6) $4.99.

(how much do you really want to know?)

Weeks of Diagnosis – day 28
– what i need to say to you.

A lift

like breathing   above

                                        the horizon line

              for once   beyond   our

Past

So, now, finally,

Oh, to get inside the throat

extract   with each polyp

                    the   tiny

                                        bits

                    of

begging
i   wished
        of   myself   on the 110 South
                                            that day
        of craving

employ
        the acumen   or   drive both of us

                                                        off
                                            that road
                                or

veer   right   into   the   wall

save
        Mercy   for another time

                                regurgitate

The

Moment.

        let it come up
                        to the surface

        the tongue

        peels apart

slip(k)not

the layers

the covers

(that)

surround

Our memorywords

the ones that abandoned your duty

just that   one time

the ones a daughter would trade in
for every happy moment of
childhood
the ones that speak too plainly of
hurting   plans
to   hurt   self
appeal to   that time   in your

car

belly full
of tantrums

the

attempt

(when i was not driving)
vanish(ed) into a wormhole of
hollow throats   then   – no.

because you
did
stop
anyway

Please remember

        only

               the key
               in

          reverse.

          On Hurting Self: i will

        say this to

you

now –

      i wish it were the other way around:

You are allowed,

But can't.

Letters of Supplication to Ma – part 1

Dear
Ma,

Remember
That
Night
You
Sat
In
Our
Room
On
The
Bed
Of
That
Old
B
&
B
Because
There
Was
No
Place
To
Sit
In
Relaxation
Only
That

Squeaky
Chair
At
The
Desk
But
I
Said
I
Needed
It
To
Work
On
Taxes
So
I
Was
Lying
I
Was
Trying
To
Write
Away
The
Day
You
Looked
Up
After
Two
Appointments

With
The
Medium
One
More
Scheduled
For
Tomorrow
Two
More
Than
We
Came
Here
For
But
It
Wasn't
enough
And
It
Wasn't
Looking
Good
Was
Starting
To
Feel
Like
Santa
Barbara
Or
Illinois

Or
Carson
Or
Internet
Or
All
Those
Other
Places
Where
We
Tried
To
Contact
The
Dead
And
Nobody
Looked
Back
At
Us
Long
Enough
And
None
Of
Them
Resembled
dad
You
Looked
Up

And
Told
Me:
Wow
My
Life
Is
Kind
Of
Crazy
I
Guess
You
Should
Write
About
This
So
Let
Me
Ma
I
Promise
To
Honor
What
We
Need
To
Extinguish

N.T.S.

1) Write a letter to your Mom:

tell her all the ways
in which you fear
disappointing her,
all the ways disease
is a good distraction
from pain.

2) Read it aloud to someone, not your Mom,

or / then

3) Burn this.

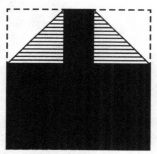

**Need Warm
Clothing**

SERIAL MEMORY – for Grandpa

7: Eminent Domain in the 50s

Crenshaw exit off the 405 in North Torrance:
1. Next door to the Coffee Bean where I write
2. Down the street from Ma's old high school
3. The exact point where the government told
   Grandpa
he would be removed from his life at their whim
he understood Eminent Domain would be explained by
muscle memory – like concentration, exclusion, war

All he could muster was the word:

Again

Concrete pillars came to plow through his blood that fed their
land and
quell the guts from the shigin he used to sing

Everything else, locked –
between a bottle of sake
and the soil in his palm,

where stone turns to ash
.
.
.
.
.

N.T.S.
When we make
pilgrimage to Manzanar
every
 April, the weeds
return to their previous
formation: blood,
 song, slivers of bone

.
.
.
.

#4: death = fault

I was 4 years-old. Grandpa came to watch me dance the
Tanko Bushi since he couldn't make it to the weekend of
the Obon in Harbor City. He brought over a big
watermelon and laughed his full face-wrinkled laugh,
while reminding me to smile as I danced the Coal Miner's
Dance, in a circle, around the living room. Grandpa left
not long after and stopped by Koda-san's house a block
away to have a few too many drinks, like always.
A couple hours later, after dinner and lots of watermelon,
I plopped on the couch next to George, who was 6 ½ at the
time. He was the favorite grandkid - he was always
amenable, always game, always enjoyed anything
Grandpa put in front of his face to eat. That made no
sense to me. I hated everything except mochi and plain
spaghetti noodles.

Then, we got the call. The one Mom hopped up to
catch. The one when the world slowed everything into an
elastic time warp. The one with news that made Mom
jump and scream in hysterics. The telephone cord

stretched three times longer than I knew it could while mom tugged and released, running back and forth, to and from the phone attached to the wall. It looked like she was dancing in circles.

She was incomprehensible through screams from the news on the other side of the line. Someone called to say Grandpa was just a few blocks away on 235th Street, stuck in his truck, plowed through the driver's seat by a motorcyclist. Mom couldn't stop rotating through her screams, *"Pop died! Pop died! Pop is dead!"*
He was drinking. He was drinking. He had been drinking.

I understood quickly that "died" meant something bad, something gone, something away, something like the smell of smoke, steel and noise.

George turned to me and said,
"You know, this is your
fault."

I looked at him and for once something made sense.
Grandpa did come all the way here to watch me dance. And bring me a big watermelon. And remind me to smile. And now he was stuck, or gone, just three blocks away on Western and 235th.
As plainly as we sat on that couch, my feet dangling well above the floor, I looked at my brother and nodded,

"...okay."

N.T. George:
It's okay.
You were
only 6. And
he was your
favorite, too.

N.T.S.
I never attempt
a left turn onto
Western
            from 235th.

.
.
.

#40: the country club

I once met a wealthy nurseryman who gave credit to my
Grandpa for giving him his first job at a nursery. Mom and I
met with him and his daughter, at a beautiful home in New-
port Beach. Or was it Laguna Nigel? I was excited to hear
more of his memories from when he was a much younger
man at the Kato Nursery. He was nice enough to meet with
us and take us to lunch at his country club. His daughter came
along - a hip and cool mama with short, jet black and spiky
Sansei hair and clothing with labels I could tell I didn't rec-
ognize. And black and white sneakers that were undercover
bling. (You can always tell with the shoes.)
I remember the daughter talking about her daughter's
entrepreneurship. She was the only one of her friends brave
enough to peddle Girl Scout cookies at their high school. She
ended up selling so much to all the kids with their sizeable,
disposable allowances that she herself made thousands for her
commission. I realized I had no
prior knowledge that Girl Scouts made a commission.

The old man nodded along the telling of this story, proud of his granddaughter's business savvy. We were into the main course and he still hadn't offered up stories about my Grandpa, so I finally asked for some. He took his time, and in between bites, he said:

He drank so much!
He drank all the time.
In between customers, he
went behind the cash register –
He had a bottle back there!

And he'd drink!

Then he returned to his lunch.
I remember everyone kept looking down, kept eating. I remember wanting to ask if there were other memories, but I didn't dare stop chewing. And the salmon was tougher than it should have been for what it must have cost.

And the granddaughter bought wells in Cambodia with her commission.

I cannot remember anything else.
.
.
.
.
.

#43, circa 1958: The Auction

Mom never told me this part

    They didn't just come to sell him on Eminent Domain
    They came, mouths slobbering, all official, regurgitating
    an old memory, familiar language pinned to new
    cufflinks in starchy button-downs

No one to explain why time stopped
whenever the white man arrived
at his nursery in a suit and a cheap smile, armed
with the gift of shock-but-no-surprise

No one to explain the definition of Fair Market Value
        for
Land already potted in their blueprints and back pockets
Soil drunk with his sweat
A future of concrete bones already stuck in his past
His head muddled by their myths

    removal on repeat:

    Again.

Grandpa's only utterance
    when it came to the government
Their only offering
    when it came
        Again. Again. Again.

But

Then they said

he could keep his house
cut from the foundation
and moved to land
there were no plans for

Ma said

But

Pop was a Kagoshima man
Heavy workers
Hard drinkers
Bad tempers

He said

        Take it all
        Take the land
        Take the house

    (Took the house)

Until some weeks later
he decided they should
untake it

       I need my house

His voice, a rumble of disqualified
words, traveled across the desk
of the county office
(did the clerk even look up?)

They said

Your house, is up for auction, there
is nothing we can do, show
up next week to
bid for the house, try
and win it back

> (N.T.S.
> This is where I wanted to   stop
> the memory from speaking,
> wanted to lean on that Kagoshima
> anger, stew
> in denial for a minute on how
> all offerings from the government
> end

> *Grandpa – let your Kagoshima pride lift your head up*
> *long enough for them to look you in the eye,*
> *then leave them there,*

> *Deny them your gifts of*
> > *hope*
> > *Stop speaking, Ma, the story must end here*
> > *My breathing only has space for*
> > > *contempt)*

Two weeks later
Grandpa took the whole family
to go bid on themselves

They waited inside, hovering like
ghosts visiting their own home
while
he went out there, heavy
hands tucked into vast pockets

Of course
the auction didn't last, didn't let anyone breathe
long breaths, held them there, long enough
to make sure his
were the last
to leave
Grandpa   emerged,   chin down, face showing

                    the price
          of the house he lost
for a second time

                    And now the wind had gone and placed
                    a two foot hole in my ability to forget

I drove a few miles southwest to go and stare
                    at the freeway exit on Crenshaw
                in search of the moment
          that
     made him
vanish long before his death

                    Never to see the look on his
                    face that I swear I can't get
                    out
                    of
                    my
                    head

.
.
.
.
.

#0: memory ground zero

There can't be anymore of these
i thought i was done extracting history from our flesh, we are still
uncovering shrapnel embedded in our memory, stuck
in a
trial
where *remembering* is just another way of knowing –

in this country,
                we are here to survive
                        a series of heartbreaks

Can i get a good one?
Can i be surprised next year with a great story mom
forgot to share?

How about a time Grandpa came home, smile beaming clear
across the living room and that was the reason he wanted to
reach for the bottle that day? And who knows why? Who
knows?

Someone must know something – say, of an unannounced
sum of money returned to him from that old buddy who we
once called thief, but turned out to be a comatose samaritan
who just needed a few extra decades to repay Grandpa.
Something happy,
                wonderful,
                        magnificent like that would have been nice to
have happened. Maybe it did happen? Who knows?

Not that I need to know this for me

And this is not for him or his redemption

Not to restore faith into this country or his faith into this
country or anything into this country,
I don't want to expect to need anything more out of this
country.
I just need a surprise. And a good memory. One that prom-
ises it lived before me. That it had time to seep into our
bones. Some event – that sprung...and leapt...and flew so
high beyond grandpa's expectations of one amazing
moment...that when he, in his last beats of breath, in
that truck, on that road, had that one time to look back
on, and so could exhale – through fumes of gas, stench of
alcohol, ripped metal, and burnt blood – one thought
emerged in homage to that moment so sweet he never
bothered to tell anyone that it ever happened, but it did.
And then he died.

I need someone to tell me that.

I need someone to place something in my hands
Some measure of worth beyond the graves
we have tried not to abandon
All we have is ash

I want bone
Big, thick bones
Let me place them
at the makeshift altar on every surface of my bookcase

There:

Uncle Jim's elbow joint, holding those chapbooks together;

There:

Bachan's teeth rounding out the graphic novels;

Dad's jaw clipped over the songbooks;

Grandma's clavicle in between the Buddhist book of death
poems and the Student Bible (can't you hear her laughing?)

And there:

                    Grandpa's wrist bone
                split, a flayed rosebud atop the stack of
obituaries on the second shelf

                    Grandpa's kneecap
                pressing our storyline into the pages of
Unknown Historical Records

                        Grandpa, carpal and metacarpal
                    on the bottom shelf – to supply us with
roots, bloomed and stone, unfettered
                    release ash from its grip
                    resist the traitors of sanity
                    take back what our nights whisper we
                    needed to

survive:

> *love, stoic – hide all acknowledgments;*

> *hearts, distal – situate yourself away from your*
> *center;*

> *memory, interred – ancestral remains, buried in*
> *marrow.*

Letters to Taz

*(after Taz Ahmed's "If Our Grandparents Could Meet –
dedicated to my JA allies")*

Dear Taz,

I hope this finds you in spirits
unlike my own.
I have tried in vain to find more on the
stories you seek of your family –
why does research of our ancestors
feel so unromantic? So disappeared?
Please no one say to me again you
can find everything on the internet,
that fraud of a storyteller with no soul.
Why do our pages not come to us
on carriage or horseback or chins
tilted upward with purple
pink golden sunsets in the
background visage they left behind?

I find bits and bytes of information
that build a shell of a structure
too sterile to house your family's truths.
Why are our pages not pages at all?

Where are the voices that interlace
the iron gates with
records of trains that move past the
point of what maps have been drawn?
Where are the memories – split
by the wire that surrounded them,
burdened with more weight
than what they could carry?

Where are the
remnants
of
their proudest
echoes
being
stored?

I am feeling wretched
as we are left to merely
imagine the holes
and fill the memory
and surmise the blankness.

If it is any consolation –
once in a while,
and only a very spare while –
I can't help but find it might be better this way.
With every tale we trace
over eons,
from reluctant kin,
With every notice of heartbreak
we extract from bone and grave,
skin and soil,
how luscious in fact it is
to find less,
hear less,
know less.

When a memory that is old
and belongs to the dead only
makes their moment of crushing
land like a rusted nail
at the tip of my tongue.

That lost son. That never meeting. All those babies dying as babies and then again as adults. That turned cheek. That hidden bottle behind the cash register. That snickering hand. That taking and taking and taking again. That last sip. That time and again starvation. That hole in the ground underneath their trustful feet.

I suck back the acid, clench these stories
with my teeth, keep them with me –
there is nowhere I trust to spit them out.
My body is in constant debate on
whether to forbid
their release.

Do you ever feel this?
I suspect this is a taste you, too,
know too well.

I hold you with me, keep me with you.

tkk

**Should We Wait
For Rescue Plane?**

December 7

That fierce mother of mine
was all of ninety pounds
in her early twenties while
etching English and Nihongo
lessons upon eager minds
at Monroe High School
in the Valley

She was stern, serious
spent every ounce of
attention on
curriculum, every part of her
pocketbook and social life
on the students, no
surprise she ended up
being everybody's favorite

This day, in the 60s,
was "Kill-A-Jap Day,"
each year the same, but
news to her in that first year
of teaching so there it came
to greet her through
steel teeth one morning

The announcement of
said infamous day cast
over loudspeakers right into
the classroom like a tinny
gray cloud, those knowing
grins prematurely detonated
before all eyes shifted
to their beloved teacher

Unsteady hands slipped
around sweaty chalk,
the room steadfast in
collective breathlessness,
as if their exhale would be
the final blow against
the back of her knees

They never thought much
about what was simply
how it always was, but
in a moment, Room 25
at Monroe High was
silenced by the pause
hanging above two tiny feet
at the front of the room

Never before had they
witnessed a posture
buckle by the shock of
watching her own spirit
become a shadow of itself

It was in an instant, surely,
when that day became one
they would never forget

No Redress

(dedicated to ALL the ancestors who died before knowing that Redress & Reparations would be a thing to come or to be fought for in the future we call now)

no museum

no monument

no poem
no song
can house
the spirit
of a passed soul
like that of my
grandfather
who died before
justice
could meet
the old man
at his mailbox

Grandpa
never got to
stand in line
at the bank
three inches
taller
with Redress check
in hand
one foot in front

of the other
feeling
grounded again

never got to deposit
an apology
in
his savings account

never got to wonder
of how he might
spend
this money
on new equipment
for the nursery or
a truck for himself or
college money for
his grandchildren
or
for once
take
the most
takai cuts
from the fish truck man

most years
in April

I attend
Pilgrimage

I say
Hello, Manzanar

I bow at the graves

I speak to the wind
of my hopes
for
Afterlife
to be a real thing

not so I can see
Grandpa again

but for him
to look around today, jump
into the circle, dance
the Tanko Bushi
and watch
me get it right

and see our friends
all our relations
learn what we mean by
chosen family
we are here

not only to remember

but to remind the local docents
this place will never
be a museum

this body will never
forget

and we leave Pilgrimage
with pledges as concrete
as the monument

we sing songs
to keep each other awake
on the long ride home

we lose sight quickly
rearview mirrors
a pitch black sky

where they close the gate
at the hour
they have had enough of us

where we leave behind
parts of our
best poetry

where I hope not
but
think
grandpa
sits
still
waiting

Last Time in D.C.

Bachan's great fake teeth
Around my mother's chocolate cake
A birthday gift from her daughter-in-law

Tongue between
A million wrinkles
Turned upward
Bachan commanded:

Half for her
And the rest
Sliced into tiny pieces to be shared
By all other celebrants

The only time every year
She would allow for
Selfishness

A woman of no other declaration
For wanting
We savored this annual claim
Her gift to us

When she returned from Washington D.C.
In October that year
We took our last photograph

Together at LAX
Side by side in wheelchairs
Me, from that car accident

Her, from being old and
looking ahead to year 101

It was time to plan for
Another grand bout with
Birthday cake

But this time she was already satisfied
She received the ultimate gift
One of the last surviving Issei
Flown in to receive apology
On a stage with dozens of cameras
There to capture the
Flash of her smile
Hands locked in prayer, in gassho

She proclaimed that D.C. was
The Best City in the World
Lavished with Redress check,
An official reparation from
The government,
And their final present held in a small red box

She gave this to my father to give to me
He, the youngest of her children
Me, the youngest of her grandchildren
Still, it must be a
Secret
This,
A precious bracelet of solid gold!
You must keep it in a secure place
She said
It must be worth a lot of money
Because it came from the government

Near salivating, impatient,
When no other aunties, uncles and cousins
Were looking
I pried open the box to see
Bachan's latest treasure

I held it out to the light
Held it close
Something about its color,   brass
Something about its weight,   hollow
Something shouted to me to   run to another room
To have a closer look

Across the clasp
In capital letters
A V O N

Avon
Like the makeup catalogue sitting on mom's credenza
Filled with cheap perfume and salmon colored
Lipstick that
Never looked quite right in the light

Costume jewelry
Sat in my palms
Sweating, burning,
Lying

There
The temptation to crush this into crumbs
Against the wall
Because it would feel so good and

Because it would be too easy to do so
But it was not mine,
Will never be mine

In secret
I promised to return for her
Someday
To this city of her favor

Spit out
Brass-plated
Metal shards
I have held under my tongue all these years

Gather myself in her proclamations of forgiveness
Swallow, whole pieces of her wanting
Exist here, with her last exit
And somehow,
Taste sweetness again
But for her
Only for her

Letters to Taz – on meeting

(after Taz Ahmed's "If Our Grandparents Could Meet")

Dear Taz,

And what if we had been able to
introduce our grandparents?

Would we have endured the summer heat
to dance in honor of our ancestors and
understand our proximity to
tradition versus survival?

Would they agree to disagree
on the presence or void of gods?
Would they respect the sufficiency
of saying less in order to hold
the future between us?

And I wonder of the simplest things:
Did your grandma have a hearty laugh?
Did your grandpa also like to drink?

It would've been fun to see them squat
against the sun
and share the shade
of their fleeting respite

And exchange bits of wisdom
in meditations, chants, and duas

And trace back the steps
before the wire

And take in the wine
of better memories

And offer each other permission
to voice a wild dream

And yell towards the devils
of another man's heaven

And trust that their memories
would rattle the bones
of their granddaughters

And speak of children who
would someday make them proud

And know, without fail or the need for faith,
that their future
really did have something to
look forward to.

in kinship,

tra

**Need Quinine
or Atabrine**

club so hot it turned December into sticky hot coal summer
in the upper floors of the Variety Arts Center.
heat rising, too many fights breaking, shut down, got too
hot, too bad, I didn't even get to dance. exit fast,
not fast enough. something smells bad.
eyes lock, bad. heat, bad. 18&over-cheap-cover want so bad
to fight,
bad.
whatchu lookin at bitch, bad. keep walkin, bad. pace. fast. bad.

then eight, nine, ten pairs, platform-heeled surge of stones, a
handful of
kicks from their boyfriends, just for kicks. bounce. drop.
on my head, bells. my ear, rope. my back, arching heap of
rubber.
convince myself between all i can do is scream: all i am is
rubber.
then, silence, the come to, slow motion eyelids and
the shoulder blades raking the sidewalk, two pairs of hands
dragging
me
all I see is Nawa and Bryan run toward me mouthing – NO
– and
once more: bounce. drop. bounce.

bury: numbskull thoughts of revenge,
save: party flyer, fundraiser for A3M, 9th & Fig.
bury: the pirate eye, the elephant head, the battle shirt
save: hair clump in a plastic
baggy.

bury self long enough so mom & dad won't worry, won't
send me back to
Can't/ shouldn't/ don't. maybe.

Los Angeles – 1

This city is not obvious,
It is not that pretty, either

You might not parachute here
and land in amiable loveliness

For that, you will have to be
dropped off elsewhere

Pick a different metropolis
in the states

San Francisco, Chicago, Seattle,
New York, of course New York

Pick anywhere else
if you want easy or logical or sensible

If you desire accessible strolls or subways
from one neighborhood to the next

Ones where you don't constantly feel
like the lone asshole crossing the street

You can, I believe,
at just about any time of day or day of the week

Go anywhere else and walk alone in the glory
of that particularly architecturally beautiful city

I experience splendor there in those places
my eyes dancing up and down with wonder

Full of people watching, never having to actually
speak to a one, just look and walk among them

It is, some say, all they could ever want and need
and if you agree, I say

Go there
Remain there if it is most comfortable for you

Or if you must
Or if you really want to try

You can come here
You can stay a while with our lady

You cannot just visit
You must actually stay for a time

You will need wheels
You will need a map

You will need an intrepid spirit
You will need patience and time

And most of all
And, trust me, thank goodness for this part,

You will need
People

Los Angeles is not a stand-alone city

It is not in itself a jewel
It stands on the shoulders of its gems

The ones who know this city well enough
to explain the difference to starry-eyed tourists

The ones who can traverse a hipster scene and spot
the few raised in L.A. and the thousands who are not

The ones who know this city is a place that gnaws at
souls until they crack, just to see if they can take it

The ones who fight with the jaded for all they perpetuate to
fit this city, less themselves, into stereotype and slivered
screen

The ones you need to seek out and identify
if you are to survive past two days without traps

Those who are looking out for you as you are searching
for them, but you really have to mean it

The searching, that is
And once you are willing to work that hard

Then suddenly you find the gems who love you back
and loving this city becomes easy

Trust me

Obon, circa 2020 –or– Fools Dancing in a Time of Pandemic

In Los Angeles
the last Obon of the season
falls in August and settles
hundreds of festival-goers
at the Gardena Buddhist Temple
down the street from me

We have a tradition of inviting in friends
to our living room on the last day
Old-timers, new-timers and first-timers to Obon –
A season of festival and fundraising
where temples
hoist pop-up tents atop their parking lots
to host nostalgia from hoop tosses to teri chicken plates
fill each room with bake sales and ikebana demonstrations
and draw circles of chalk on asphalt
for the length of an entire block for
The Dance – the main
reason   (beyond the shave ice and spam musubi)
we come together every summer

George Abe, known in drum circles as the Moon Man,
sits on the floor of my home
Unfolds a large furoshiki to reveal
his handmade shakuhachi
And through breaths of flute and song
he talks story of why
we bring the fools watching
into the fold of the fools dancing
Here we are not afraid to speak about death
Here we gather to honor the dead
Here the spirits sway among us

This year, I dance in my living room to virtual Obon
gatherings
The names of those we lost swirl in my head

I look forward to next year with eager hopes
for us to return in person

But for now
I miss
the friends streaming through the door

I miss stuffing the little ones –
Addie, Bobbi, Simone, Eka & Skye –
each into fluffy obi and toddler-sized happi coats

I miss our group walk across 162nd Street and
down Denker Avenue to the Temple

I miss the hoarding of spam musubi
into my fanny pack

I miss the kernels of corn stuck to my cheek

I miss the bingo at the end of the night
Smiling like winners in our sea of losing cards

And I miss the first dance at 6:00pm –
Bon Odori Uta, where I begin
to sing the names of those who've died

And I miss my joyous 360 degree spin with the 1+1

And I miss saying hello to Grandpa
as we dig coal during the Tanko Bushi

Round and round
in concentric circles up and down
Halldale Avenue

We twirl around the neighborhood

a collective of bodies
in axis with the earth

The universe expanding its breath
around us
with us
into us

And we are not afraid to think on dying
here we dance for the dead
here we dance with the dead

bloody, near bloody

all I remember
at times

of that time

is a pile of hair

in a heap
in the palm of my hand

after bouncing around
like a basketball, Bryan said
they bounced you around
like a basketball

he said
what you're doing to your hair
I wasn't sure if it was a question
or the beginning of an observation

but it didn't matter
and sometimes you
don't say much when
you're in the passenger seat
of a friend's car, hoping that
whatever hospital he takes
you to
has an ER
that will let you in

when you
notice your head is starting
to morph into
another shape
and you catch yourself
in the mirror of the
car visor:
a rapid time-lapse
of a blood flower swelling
in midsummer

not much came to matter when
I was on the way to some
Emergency Room with
a blossoming head
and a pile of hair
in my hands

in my hands
what I was doing with my hair
was combing it out like I used to
fingers full of strands that
I'd pile onto
my father's desk, webbed
like a tumbleweed, the
size
of a basketball

Dad came upstairs once and asked
me what the hell was I doing
trying to pull out all of my hair

I didn't know how to answer
I wasn't trying to do that,

as much as I hadn't
planned to,
just as surely as
those girls
didn't begin their
evening,
earlier tonight,
with a wait Downtown in line at
the 18-&-over club,
and a plan
to pull at my hair

pull at my hair
a part of me
did wonder
if that's why it was so thin

or if I'd show patches
of skin when all was said and
done

it did flash in my head that I was
done
during the barrage of a dozen feet
batches of kicks from their
boyfriends on the side
bouncing around the
sidewalk in that
tug-of-war between
feet to my lower back
and fingers entwined
like climbing vines at
the top of my
head

they are flashes now
moments
between
mayhem and bounty
between
too much cool and
too much heat
between beat drops
and shut downs
between long waits to exit
and all the people
waiting to fight
between the guys
trying to pull
each one off of me
while trying
to defend
themselves
between
gravel and ivy
fence and sport
punch and party
screams and chambers
drag and capture
waiting and stitches
bloody and near bloody

I rarely think about it anymore
when I'm on 9th & Fig
not nearly as often as I did
in those days when I
kept avoiding
9th & Fig

but once in awhile
my mind takes walks
that way
when my fingers
get caught
in my tangles

when I pull more than I should

when I see small piles
of hair
bouncing around
or

lying on a sidewalk
in a heap

N.T.N.

Los Angeles Drives, part 1

take
the 18-minute
drive from Gardena to
Highland Park on a Sunday
morning and this city will show
she can still host you with some grace

.
.
.

I miss living in
Eagle Rock
if only for my four
favorite ways of getting home

the best:

take
San Fernando
off of Avenue 19 from Spring
at the 24 Hour Michoacan,
enjoy those hills, the tracks,
the underpass, ride like you
think you're cool, zipping a right –
and change it up each time –
on any of the tiny streets that

get you to Eagle Rock Boulevard,
try not to stop for pan de sal every time,
and right on York, to
land at the intersection
of the fire engines and frat houses,
the night birds and the mack trucks
barreling down the boulevard
that lulled me
to sleep on my tiny balcony on
summer nights,
oh, that beautiful cacophony –
the sounds that make me forget the
noisy drama of a younger life

.

.

.

If you watch too many films like
CRASH or LA STORY, you might
never believe there are entire volumes
of less spoken truths on driving in
this city.

I'll tell you one story – my friend Sefa
takes care of a whole bunch of young
people on the job over an hour from
home, where he takes care of a whole
lot of family with his family.
That one hour to work and back –
with his CDs and yes,
people still use CDs and he has his
special stack, curated better than
your Spotify playlist –
that is his personal den, his private
karaoke box,

his
time.

There's the other side of road rage –
where I catch up, conference call,
rehearse lines, head write, take naps
between meetings, do accounting,
pull over (or not) and actually write,
public radio, podcast, audiobook through
traffic.

In LA, you have to get crafty with
the bullshit.

This is sometimes my only
me time.

This
is
Road Joy.

Los Angeles is (such) a Scorpio

No, don't try to convince me with its Virgo assignment at
birth.
You want to know how I know LA is a Scorpio?

I / You
(you live here long enough and then travel out of town, then
likely You at some point)
(definitely I)
meet someone
usually somewhere not here,
in the company of that person's longtime or born-and-raised
living place,
and as soon as they ask
"Where'd you come in from?"
I can barely say "Los Ang/"
and there they go:
People
make all kinds of assumptions about us,
passing judgment
brimming with assumption, fixed ideas,
and increasingly negative narratives.

And then you realize a half hour into the conversation
they've never spent more than a weekend or two,
more than a Disneyland trip or stop in Santa Monica
or the Venice boardwalk or Sunset Strip
or maybe Chinatown, but really just Far East Plaza,
nowhere anywhere close to the bones of our arena, nope,
nope, nope.

Just like that time an ex had screamed into the phone
upon learning I am a Scorpio
that they don't fuck with Scorpios,
ever.

What's your sign anyway, San Francisco?

N.T.S.
Okay, at the very least, LA's Neptune has got to be in
Scorpio.

The Continuum: in the path of the greater good

For The Invisible Capes of J-Town

Always in someone's way.
Always a piece of us.
       delicious. little. tokyo. appetizer.
Looking good once we started looking good.
Always moving, always being moved.

Order: nowhere else but an enclave. here. move. sit. stay.
         hurry. wait. go. do not gather. do not return.

Dig: City Hall hungry – raze. push. grab. raze.

Shove: wartime incarceration infatuation – raze. raze. raze.
         raze. raze. Jim said it was meant to be *extermination*
         raze. raze. raze.
         raze.

Squeeze: Kajima corporation ravenous - set the Sun. raze.
         push. grab. move the old people. again.

Sneeze: Arts District thirsty – take. grab. fake. take. name.
         name. name.

Repeat: repeat. repeat. repeat.

Welcome Basket: *Everyone is welcome in Little Tokyo, but please*
                          remove your shoes at the door.

Past – Night

J-Town in the 90s:

for the art+community of Tuesday Night Café

Open: PRC on Avenue 57. The World Stage. Self-Help
        Graphics.

Open: inspiration all around. parallel worlds. art.
        community. people.

Open: looking for queues. and cues. and clues.

Open: a question. what's going to happen to J-Town.

Open: three or four joints after 10:00p. a sheen of
        washed out amber grey.

Open: a question. what's our scene. an Asian American
        scene. where?

Open: a courtyard.

Open: hearts. Visual Communications. East West Players.
        our little engine that could.

Open: more questions. what else? what more? what
        next?

Open: an organization. a service center. a community
        development group.

Open: roots in serving the people. Evelyn says:
        We've always needed art in the movement.

Open: art. service. we could be a form of community
        development.
Open: a nodding head with roots in radical action.

Open: Evelyn says: *Little Tokyo needs more people now.*

Open: talking to more people. more nodding heads.

Open: Evelyn says: *Let's go talk to Bill.*

Open: match in hand. sandpaper on the ground. Bill says
        Go. Try. Build.

Open: take the days. take the weeks. take all the
        conversations possible.

Open: the question. the need. the people. respond.

Open: Mitsuru Grill for meetings. Oiwake for the
        buffet+karaoke. Suehiro for 1am.

Open: take the months. but start. make the mistakes
        that need to be made.

Open: a dozen pairs of swift feet. beg, borrow, steal.

Open: hands on chairs, wiping. hands on tables, tugging.
        hands on deck, all.

Open: Daryl's got the cans. I got the mic – nope, not
        saying from where.

Open: Gerry brought the Leko's & Fresnells. Glenn has
        the mixer. what more?

Open: Tuesday Night. what next?

Open: make it free. no green room. no backstage. open
        alleyways. no one-ways.

Open: pre-show toast with Johneric at Cosmos. (no
        sleeping in the booths post-show)

Open: tag team with Rona on the order. who else wants
        to perform?

Open: inspiration with a side of Melissa's smile, Cindy's
        snark, and Amelia's bread pudding.

Open: what do we call this thing. who cares. just start.

Open: on constant rotation sweet as a Visiting Violette.
        here. and. now.

Open: Eddie's shutter. stack of pictures every 2 weeks
        from Kimura Photo. caption: 90012

Open: need. art. place. art. people. art. space. art.
        move. art plus community one thing.

N.T.S.
When creating a space, know that you are co-creating.
Co-create a space of self-determination that can be
sustainable for the long haul. Bring in as many as want
to be in – each taking on a small task of the whole.
Reject the "Superwoman" fallacy. Lean in to each
person's expertise, craving, and curiosity.

N.T.S.

When (co)creating a space, always ask of self
and the team: What is the win-win-win-win-win?
How does the artist win in an effort that is grassroots and
all-volunteer? How will you do your best to make sure they
look good, sound good, feel good onstage, and more
importantly, before and after the "event."
How are we building relationships and genuine support in
the long-term?
How does the audience win? Who is the audience? Who is
in the room?
Who is not in the room?
How does the community win? Who is present? Who is
past?
Who is future?
How does the larger world around us win, even if they
never know we exist?
How does the team win?
The generous crew of folks who go out of their
way, many never to take the stage, to ensure all of the above
feel the wins.

Present – Da(il)y
J-Town:

1) photoshoots.

2) lines.   a faster clock.

3) tension.   rising.
some remember to remove their shoes at the door.

                                   some keep
                                   forgetting. on
                                   purpose.

                    4) cosplayers.
sometimes a whole group. sometimes one in a group. No
                                   convention
                                   necessary.

5) The Invisible Capes.

6) no more free

parking.   (meters feeding our trees

                                   streets

                                   hungry friends and

                                   neighbors?)

7) a community combat council
   = a sigh of relief.

8) the few secrets left we will try to
   keep.

The Invisible Capes of Little Tokyo

You've seen them

But you may be distracted by the obvious:
The kids in cosplay – attire in homage to beloved characters of
the Manga world
They come to Little Tokyo to feel free to
be their inner anime spirit
Some in homespun costume with cardboard staff and older
sibling graduation gown
Others heed to $400 corset with tulle petticoat and platform
Mary Jane's

I watch the tourists request photos with the best dressed
It is not Halloween
This is any day of the week
No Anime Con necessary

The intersection is complex
A safe haven for the misfits of other parts of the city
and
A year-round open-season Japanophile-fantasyland

But the richest scene
comes when I stop and consider
the less seen
My main attraction:
            The J-Town OGs

The Little Tokyo Superheroes

The Ordinary Extraordinary
who carry my history in their pockets and
memories of when their attendance
was undeterred by the dismal numbers
roaming about past 6pm

I swear I see it all the time:

The Ghosts of J-Town Past
high-fiving the
Little Tokyo Pros of the Present –

The ones with shooting stars in
the shape of two tennis
balls guiding the front of a walker
The
Nisei volunteers walking back to the museum
with seed packets from Anzen Hardware
and pride more complicated than war
The
70-something community organizer with a stack
of meetings on her shoulders, the weight of battle at
her ankles, and *I Don't Give a Fuck* written all over her face
The
Young Blood building pipelines along 2nd Street, entry
points on Judge John Aiso, bridges this side of the Towers,
for
the next generation of youth...and the next and the next

Around their necks, they
wear invisible capes the
size of parachutes

Armed with staff & sword in the form of plastic file carriers
from Daiso
and treasure maps of the 4 x 6 cardstock kind
Donning satchels of Bokashi compost and
Elixir of Sake or espresso
Walking the cultural spine through pumpkin patches
Hanging with the wolves, cranes, and kings who share their
loot with the whole lot

The next time you're in Little Tokyo
Walk down First Street.

                     Turn your head. Look up.

An Invisible Cape.   Another one just
                                                  passed you by.

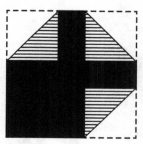

**Need First-Aid
Supplies**

N.T.S.
Humans really like to take over
shit once it seems safe or cheap
enough to do so.

(for whenever)
you might need a character:

FUMIKO
Breakdown:

Uniform 1: black mohawk; knee high black CAT
construction boots; black leggings; black turtleneck.

Uniform 2: black bob; black heels; black shirt dress with
black obi; eyeglasses with black frames.

Pronouns & ways to address: she / they / F

Prop: carries sign that reads, "Welcome to Little Tokyo.
Remove your shoes at the door."

Emotional Character -
How does the character deal with:

1.Anger   -> anger is a tasty morsel inside Fumiko's
                 mouth. F takes great pleasure in sharing it
                 with the world.

2.Change   -> change coming from an external force that excludes Fumiko's sense of self-determination can lead F to near breakdown or explosion.

3.Sadness   -> Fumiko does not like to show their emotions in the realm of sorrow. They will usually flee the scene as swiftly as possible or attempt to internally morph the sadness into grave anger. (see Anger.)

4.Loss   -> Whenever Fumiko witnesses loss of community self-determination in Little Tokyo and Los Angeles, she experiences a cold sweat, a hollowing in her body, and a stone that emerges, simultaneously growing and disintegrating at the back of her throat.

5.Conflict   -> Fumiko sees every piece of conflict as an opportunity. F believes conflict is a constant and not enough confrontation to battle it. F therefore has great admiration and respect for the diehard fighters and pro-People practitioners who go out of their way to speak up and protect communities, history, land, spiritual ties, and means of safety, good health, and dignity. Fumiko has an especially deep place in their heart for people who do this with respect to universe and beings, past, present & future, as interconnected with all Others. F's internal conflicts are a fear of abandonment and being alone in the fight, and worries about her abrasiveness in relation to being truly effective, and worse, being left behind by the people with whom she holds in such high regard.

N.T.S.
Humans really like
eggs.

(for whenever)
you might need a song:

EGGS (lyrics)

My mama made me eat eggs
My daddy did too
My brother really loved eggs
So i stuck them in his shoe

Scrambled
Boiled
Sunny side up
Runny
Deviled
Over easy
Go and throw it up!
Aaaaaaaaaaaaaaaaaaaaaaa!

Fleshy pillows
Orange Bins
Up to my chin
Buffet style
Eggs Gone Wild
Made my belly thin

Scrambled
Boiled

Sunny side up
Runny

Deviled
Over easy
Go and throw it up!
Aaaaaaaaaaaaaaaaaaaaaaaaaaaaaaaa!

(go into crowd, try to find a person
who hates eggs too, high five them,
return to mic)

N.T.S.
Humans really don't like
talking about
menstruation.

(for whenever)
you might need a monologue:

PINK PLASTIC
(Version: age thirty-something)

I'm sitting in my favorite
stall
at my favorite
bathroom
at work
and I look down and notice
how perfectly I've placed
a fresh pad
in my underwear
--why don't I like saying "panties"?--

but I realize
I could have saved the new one for later
the old one's not that soaked-in
I have to conserve my pads today
because I don't remember how many
I have left in my backpack
--I wonder if there's a sanitary standard for
how many times a day we're supposed to change these
things?--

so I roll up the old pad
and place the backing around it
and put it in the wrapper,
this wrapper is pink.
why the hell is it pink?
---now other brands
have finally come out with
pad packaging in
all kinds of colors
but my favorite is
stuck in this funky mauve rose pink---
as if we need a distinction
from the monthly blood-cycle mini diaper that dudes wear??

i'm sitting here
thinking about my moon, my period, my flow
and i realize that i've been
on my period for over
30 years

how many pads have I used in that time???

what if we collected all the pads I ever used!
what if we collected all the pads of the nation!

and put them into one landfill!
what would that look like?
--I know what the hell that would smell like--

a sea of pink plastic
seagulls circling
they'd fly in for miles
'cuz you know this landfill would have to be
in some location WAY deep in the central east

what a mess
yes

all that fuss
all that time
all these years
my body has been making way
for potential procreative purpose
and here I am reaching the closing window
time is running out
I might never get pregnant
and make use of this whole period thing

that's crazy
that would be such a waste
that would be so sad

maybe that's why our bodies make us go
through things like this
a monthly reminder
so we don't go too long without thinking
about it

like I have to have something to
show for all this

hassle
well.
I guess.
it IS more than a hassle and cramps

and dumb plastic packaging
because,
YES

I
have been
substantially CLEANSING
releasing toxins
once a month
every year
for over three decades
and that is FANTASTIC

it is a major thing that keeps us cycling,
regenerating, healing
...that is the problem for dudes
they have no way to cleanse, release
and they get clogged
and stuck
and stuffed up
and I have to bet this is really why we
live longer than they do

well
it's just another month
another period
another year
and one more pad
for my gigantic pink plastic landfill

N.T.A.A.A.C. – On the Asian American Red Carpet
(for V.C.)

The Asian American Red Carpet is the most thirsty, the
most absorbent.
It is the elephant's elephant of Arts & Entertainment
memory.

When the other carpets start opening up to you, please
continue to love it.
Donate to it.
Don't forget about it on your way up. And even if you do,
it will still be here for you during any weird stints of time
when
and if you're not getting as much work and the other carpets
start to
roll themselves back up as you arrive.
And even after every mainstream flick or Netflix gain,
The Asian American Red Carpet will likely still be there,
taking new risks, trying on new colors, building up new
artists,
forgiving our mistakes and disappearances,
welcoming you back home.

N.T.theQuestioning-of-Self-Artist:

My friend – let's call him Apple – once told me, "Hey tra,
I've been wanting to tell you something...I think I'm gonna
quit music." Felt like a confession from someone who felt
like he was letting himself or me or the world down. He
said he tried, but just couldn't sustain himself and wished
he knew how to be a full-time artist – but since he couldn't
figure it out, it was probably time to just give it up, for good.
Apple had made a few albums, tried to do as many gigs as
would have him, but he didn't feel like he was a "success."
Through practicing art as a career and helping to build an
art+community organization called Tuesday Night Project
for so many years, I can not even tell you how many times I
have had versions of this very conversation. I've taken in
countless lamentations of "I am not that successful" and
"I'm just a part-time artist" and "I'm not a real artist" all
the while creating some of the best or most beautiful Art
I've ever experienced. My most honest answer to Apple was:
*My friend, you couldn't quit music if you tried. Maybe you
mean you need to quit the business...for now, for a while, or
in ways that continue not to work. Maybe you need to figure
out the ways it will work for you...your music, that is. Your
Art.* It's true – if you're active in artistic circles and engaged
with community enough, it can often feel like most everyone
around you has the best deal or contract or label or publisher
or platform or social media prowess or show or role or tour
or or or. That everyone is getting work. That everyone is
Famous. That everyone is Successful. But the thing is
even people you know – who are making every penny solely
from their artistic careers without another job or side gig –
they have had to bust ass while getting lucky and making
sacrifices that most of them won't ever tell you about. They

have had to pay their dues and say No to so many things just to keep their integrity intact, all the while very much knowing they are incredibly lucky and they must be extremely grateful. At the same time – many folks have figured out a hybridity of pursuits for artistic survival – like an emcee, building a life with their kids and super supportive, gainfully-employed partner, making their own videos, hosting shows, teaching workshops, speaking on panels, writing essays, taking production assistant jobs, all the while realizing they thrive and seek out and love the variety of their experience. And even still at the same time, there are whole swaths of others whose pursuit of an art practice means having a 9-to-5 and doing art at other available hours or through intensives over long weekends or retreats they take at different times of the year. One of my favorite writers ever worked full-time at 1-800-Dentist and that never stopped him from doing great Art. He did it at his own pace and on his own time and I don't think his tempo or output would necessarily change all that much, even without the full-time, Monday-through-Friday job situation. Over the past 25 plus years, I've traveled through all of these situations in various ways and have witnessed this all around me with Artists in every field. The thread that binds it all is - these are all folks who can't stop doing their Art.

And for all the folks struggling – with calling or considering themselves an Artist, or with Fame & Fortune (or lack thereof), or with the ebb-and-flow of various sectors & industries and availability or accessibility of work – please, by all means, remember this:

• You love Art? You go to Art to process? You utilize Art to communicate with the world and with yourself? You can't – in all honesty – imagine not doing Art for a second or indefinitely or a prolonged period of time?
YOU ARE AN ARTIST. SAY IT. TELL OTHERS.
Make business cards if you need to. OWN IT.

• Let go of the trappings from external forces trying to define for us, or society at large, what it means to be a "real artist" or "full-time artist" or "Artist" period.
Never diminish yourself or what you do based upon someone else's definition or expectation. OWN IT.

• Fame is an illusion. Or as Bruce said it – "The word superstar really turns me off and I'll tell you why, because the word star, man, is an illusion." BRUCE mutthafukin' LEE said this. Do not let money or Fame dictate your degree of Success – allow your definition of Success to be Self-Determined. Accolades are fleeting. Fame is relative – and more than anything, it never satisfies the call from within our Self.

I will bet money that, at the pit of the deepest core of every Artist, lies the knowledge that no amount of recognition or popularity or even respect from peers will ever provide lasting satisfaction. Feeling unsatisfied and in a constant state of questioning is part of the nature of the Artist. It roots our curiosity, as well as unsettledness. I have a high level of both. And at a certain level, thank goodness. Artists will do what they need to do to keep creating. You have to. The Artist in you needs you to do so. Indulge the curiosity and support the unsettledness so you can navigate the dissatisfaction and can keep creating.

Everyone uses the word "everyone" too much. Stop that. N.T.S. stop that.

Let us all ways feel challenged, challenging, passionate, curious, grateful, alive. Let us evaluate impact and measure our success by the process we dive into, because we've heeded our internal voice that tells us what creative risks we need to take on next. Let us listen closely to the anima that nudges us, scares us,

won't
let well enough alone.

Oh, and by the way, Apple didn't quit music.
He's been living in Ho Chi Minh City, Vietnam, raising a
kid with his partner, teaching English and music
and waiting for the right time to release his latest recordings.

N.T.S./C./W.

we are not (that) special.

                    we are not entitled to every thing.

                                        we are (not)

deserving.

                                        we
                                        are
                                        uniqu
                                        e.

                    we are hard-earned.

we are Magical Beings.

N.T.C.

Are you an artist? A writer? An art-maker? A creative?
Do you birth scripts? Novels? Poetry? Memoir?
Short Stories? Essays? Letters? Articles?
Applications? Email? Captions or comments or posts
on any social media platform? Text messages?
"Writer" or not as one of your identifiers, we all walk
through life with stories, history, experience, memories,
ideas, opinions, theories, philosophies, visions, fears,
fantasies, dreams – and will likely travel through life
holding most of these in. At some point, someone thought
it was a good idea to make record of their story or a
community's narrative. And then some of that made it
into the books you love. And some of that became the
basis for our various canons of literature. And some of that
was drawn or animated or graphic-novelized. And some of
that was made into videos, narrative films, documentaries.
And some of that was made into music. And some of that
became the thread of information we build upon in studies
of race, queerness, gender, feminism, war, history, science,
technology, and at every turn, someone at some point had
some kind of permission that became the opportunity for
them to write. Whether that opportunity was an offer to
read their writing aloud, or publish in a community
newspaper, or a voice begging from within to be processed
on paper in order to extract some deep pain or express
some kaleidoscopic vision, they all heeded permission and
need. No one will come to write your story for you or
thread together the legacy of narratives with which you
enter each room. And it doesn't matter whether you call
yourself a Writer or an Artist. What matters lies within
the doing. It is in the permission to start. So, please,
by all means, begin.

And no, not every artist gets up at 5am to start penning. And not every artist writes every damn day. You will find your own way. Just dive.

N.T.C./W. – On Creative Beings & Community Development:

All this talk of Artists and Art. Let's also be crystal clear on the nature of human as creative being, regardless of career choice. Part of my hybrid Artist Organizer career is having the privilege of working with and holding space for thousands of community builders across the country through an annual, national gathering. I get to tell stories, speak, perform, host, and facilitate alongside some amazing human beings. While it is one of my favorite partnerships that draws from many parts of my wheelhouse, the true boon underneath it all is being able to witness the work of the neighborhoods and leaders who continually remind me of what a Creative is. And why Art is not just important, it is imperative. The pandemic and lockdowns started taking over our daily consciousness in 2020, and Boom! Community organizers across the country turned to arts & culture projects, complex or simple, launching neighborhood-centered creative community gardens, or getting back to arts workshops or creative gatherings they'd been meaning for a long time to continue. Beyond the obvious inspiration abounding, the fact that this made so much sense was overwhelming. Creative practice is a way in and a way through.

People create no matter what their resources are, no matter the profession. And community builders, in particular, have an abstract yet tangible line of business through arts & culture work that invests in the arenas of mental wholeness, of emotional engagement, of historic reckoning and regeneration, of land & planet caregiving, of spiritual revitalization, of Healing.

Artivists and community development professionals have inherently connected orientations to their work: People and planet and how we take care of All and Other and Self through our most wildly inspired, timely, and deft creative collaborations.

Interstitial Palate Cleanser

Joshua Tree – day 4 of a writing retreat slowing going south

Standing over the open pizza box on the kitchen counter, stepping in place to multitask my goal for the daily walking challenge I signed up for. Already finishing the last near stale slice of The Vegan from my new favorite joint down the street. This should've lasted me at least until tonight. That's what Jaclyn said yesterday before she took off from her two day stint here, joining me at the top of this retreat. But I did give her two slices for the road and I have been reading all morning, which reeled me into the page for another set of poems I didn't come here to write. Thus the voracious nature of my break, scarfing down crust and letting the garbanzo beans and artichoke hearts fall off the side of my mouth. After I wipe down my face with the back of my hand, I'll pick up another stack of books and finish watching more videos on Jodo Shinshu and quantum physics. Then I will go and get more coffee and very likely the Buffalo Soldier (because chicken sounds good) or the Dean Martin because that had Italian sausage on it. I worry I'll never again draw out the vegetarian-vegan womxn of my twenties, who confused people at Domino's when I'd call in for a pizza with mushrooms and no cheese. Meat sounds good, sounds right, sounds like a match to ravenous writing and I already know I will be here again, taking two pieces down while standing, and stepping in place, eating like a mutthafucker. I remember when Cory said she didn't like the use of the word "motherfucker" because it sounds disrespectful to mothers. I told her I really love my mother and I really like the way "mutthafucker" sounds coming out of my mouth. Like a palate cleanser. Like the way I just need to stand and occupy my hunger over a break from writing while I try my hardest to figure out some practical application of the fourth dimension that is or is not related to a future memory of watching my mom pass through herself.

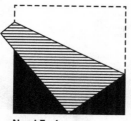

Need Tools
Plane is Flyable

Death Moment – 24

Beaudry & Figueroa Terrace was more than cheap rent.
more than my students from Castelar pinning a clock to my
door.
more than the guy telling me: *shut up if you wanna be okay.*
more than whispers: *you're gonna be okay.*

more than *Okay, shoot him* tossed behind his shoulder.
       which was the lie?
more than *who the hell did we think we were* living in
Chinatown?
more than the shiny-nail neighbors sticking too far out on
return past 1am?

Bury the target we put on our backpack, *take everything. but.*
Bury the gravel back molars, the *life did flash,* the blood
asphalt. Bury the gaze locked between my eyes and the
sidewalk.
Bury the screaming when nobody comes gonna scream
anyway.

war, near war

to measure hate, I can
say I know
love
well

I can measure fear, as I
share company with
joy and understanding
often enough

but in the scale of
war, to measure
against peace, to
measure
peace onto
itself,
we have never held
that
mirror

even in our well-lit
streets or suburban
living rooms with
plants dying on
filtered water, we
have no idea how
to mark the
end of war or
the beginning of
peace except in
moments of
forgetfulness:

forget last week's
bombings,
forget Monday through
Friday on BBC news,
forget
civilian head counts,
families still waiting
for reunion,
children still
teething underneath
rubble

in reality, is the
opposite of
war
not peace,
but instead,
amnesia?

I measure myself,
on how long I can go
with
and how long I can go
without
thinking
on
destruction,
there,
is
war

When I teach a Family & Consumer Sciences* class, this is what I say about American pie

they want me to
focus on the
exact cut i will make
for a tiny sliver to
be placed on a delicate
piece of old china

they'd like me to
pay exclusive attention
to the smallest bits
of crust for its
flakiness as we fall
off its sides,
be
grateful for the seeds
of the olallieberries,
the way they
were drowned
in thick
corn syrupy dressing

they didn't think i
would push away the slice
to concentrate
for a second
and
take a better look
at the pan and the
oven it was baked in,
then move on to the
bowl where it was mixed

at which time i will choose
to address the oven,
its temperature,
who opened it and
turned it on, who bought
the ingredients and
where they got it all from

don't proffer me
a knife when i want
to use the rolling pin,
fingers and palms circling
the flour, assessing
the foundation
beneath you

don't have me
memorize measurements
when i want to subtract
the additives and
alter all given
elements

don't give me a slice
when i want to
(re)bake the whole damn pie

*N.T.M.G.Z.F.
back in my day
they were called
Home Ec classes.
And mine were sometimes
overly gendered and weird.

And sometimes they were simply fun and nicely odd. I mostly remember baking and making cool shit with leather.

On Mass Shootings in America —or—
i felt this way 20 years ago and (sort of) can't
believe i still feel the same

We always cross our fingers that it was a White kid.

We do.

It sounds horrible, but we do.

                                        I do, anyway.

Because we know
whether it's at college
in Virginia or a military base in
Texas, Everyone will start
thinking about how the shooter
was Muslim or Korean or Black
or immigrant and right off the bat
the entire Community is thrust
into grieving two sets of loss
on both sides of the gun while
widening the eyes in the
back of their head because
they know they're in danger

Because we know
if the guy was White
no one would think twice
on whether he was Christian

or straight or cis or White
Everyone would treat the
situation like it was an isolated
incident and even though
Violence is never isolated
we wouldn't necessarily worry
about Christians or straight or cis
or White people being in danger

Because I am often like most
people and sometimes I want
things to be easy and it would
be much simpler to remember
the dead without fearing the
backlash that is sure to come
And because we are wounded
with each bullet and hardened
heart who mourns their loss
while trying to fit sense into
the nonsense of placing
blame on Difference
that keeps us all in danger

true believer

give people answers
make good and bad obvious
in their lies, your church

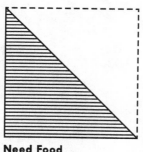

**Need Food
and Water**

Death Moment – 31

open the ground, me and ma lay down on either side.
unbury the bulging eye before you flopped back to gift final
breaths.
beg you to return in every dream, point me to the shovel,
the best soil, forgive this granddaughter and child of gardeners
for
disliking persimmons and not being able to save your lemon
tree.

unbury the superstitions, they soften my tumble into regret
never a fourth floor, never four stems, never a fourth
grandkid.
unbury the forgotten promise, the notion of no regrets,
love regret.

but to look up past their heaven to a sky of 100 billion dead,
you are in the dimension of fireside pupils who stare down
at us,
piss acid rain on our arrogance, shout toward the clock we
pummeled before it was too late.

death, near death

Death
near death

near you
at a ditch
we shoved the urn over the
side into the grave
when no one was looking

just to get it over with

it was a service
we'd been contemplating
for
nearly a week
or
months
depending on when
we admit to hiding
the real countdown
deep down
in the lowest place
between selfish organs
and guilty nerves
that refused
to ask the doctors
questions that really matter

Death
inside death

near the ditch
sometimes
I still
see her there
peeking out
from your grave

Attention

And what about the grieving widow on her way to see family, walking through the airport shortly after her loss?

If she was weeping politely, dabbing her tears as she walked, flanked by a few cousins all dressed in full regalia of mourning, wouldn't others take notice, be interested or concerned, respectfully nod their heads or even offer some help or some tissue?

But if she was walking alone, in a jagged pattern, scream-crying at a volume that matched the terror thrashing at her organs, barely able to wipe her nose with her sleeves, would others try to not look at her, pretend to not pay attention, wish she would quiet down?

Did I ever do this?

Let into recalcitrant heaving at the
first sniff of Three Flowers upon
cracking open an old jar?

Thought only of gratitude and not
at all of regret during the
middle of your annual memorium?

Sung *Love Me Tender* to the witness
of a momentarily heartbroken family?

Shouted out at the sea while a
friend hovered back on the
boardwalk to watch over me?

Fallen to my knees in front of your
grave?

N.T.W.
Notice when someone cries in public the first thing they say
is "sorry"?
Please NEVER apologize for tears. They're bits
of truth coming up for air.

on the crematorium

you will never forget
the concrete floor
and brick walls of
the crematorium, teeth
chattering
bones

your index finger
will always remember
how stiff it needed to be
against each button
of the incinerator, red,
then green, you only
came to witness, you
didn't expect to be given
this power

the inner sides of your ears
and temples
will ring
with a sudden clamor
from the securing of
a thick metal hatch
preceded by
a supreme, tender
roar upon
ignition

then you blinked
and
found yourself on
the other side of the room

squatting like a farmer to watch,
someone must have told you
to do this,
back frozen against a concrete
wall, leaning toward the flame

your body
will recall the day
it was introduced
to the
definition of
finite
as they cracked a small
opening for you to peer
into the steel tunnel
surrounding the
box, you thought
it would be fancier,
finer somehow, not
just brown cardboard with
KIRIYAMA
written on one side
with a black marker

and the fire
you will never forget
the fire
a burgeoning, orange wave
reaching out and around
you in a blanket of heat
and your skin did
not want to let go
of this embrace
and your eyes
were so

fascinated by the light
and every inch of you
jolted
into stillness
beyond
the final closure
of the chamber door
that you could not
even whisper goodbye

2 regrets

Mom and I rotated through
the ER, 30 minutes at a time

that night we had to take Dad back in
the tumor was trying to escape through his chest

My turn.

Hey Dad.
How are you?

                    I've had a good life, kid,
he said

                    I really only have
                    two regrets.

Oh yeah.
What's that?

                    We never got to take a big cruise
                    with your mom...all your
                    brothers...and Willie's kids.

I promised we could make that happen
at the time I still believed it

he was about two months from dying
but we didn't know

in the way that you also know that you do know
but don't want to know

So, what's the other thing,
Dad?

That I never got a grandchild
from you.

and I had nothing to offer but very wide eyes, an upper lip
bullying the lower against movement, and an unbelievable
inhale

Thank goodness the painkillers kicked in and after he fell
asleep,
I left the room, caught between two options:

sprint right through the walls of the hospital, past
the parking lot, and into the ether of eternal regret

or

roll around on the floor in the middle of the waiting
room, laughing uncontrollably at sanity's exit

Instead:

I walked past mom,

He's feeling better.
I have to go to the bathroom.

fathers really do know how to say the worst
goddamn things at the worst goddamn times.

N.T.S.

when you watched dad's cremation at
Oddfellows Cemetery, the crematory
operator told you the whole process would
take 10-14 hours. After the skin, hair, and
muscles vaporize and the body tissues and
bone are broken down, he lets it cool for
3-5 hours before he separates the bones. He
separated the bones. What did he do with
the bones? Did he crush them all and add
them back to the ash? Was there a
community bone pile? Could you have asked
for his bones? You wanted to ask for the
bones...even just one. Why didn't you ask for
a bone?

rain

it gets much too dry in
L.A.

so i called out for the weather to
change

or at least, i wrote to you for
it

just yesterday, as a matter of
fact

and i don't believe in
coincidence

granted, i simply acknowledged my
method

waiting for haphazard
showers

to come and clean my
car

this car i drive that once was
yours

don't think i forgot, i do vividly
recall

you relayed two simple requests to
me

time and time
again:

Keep the car
clean.

Visit me at my
grave.

i am terrible at
both.

so you answered with
rain.

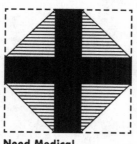

**Need Medical
Attention**

fire, near fire

Whenever we talk
In community
About Manzanar,
Or Tule, or
Internment, or
American
Concentration
Camps,
We often hear
About the dust,
The irrigation by
The hands of the
Japanese farmer,
The bitter winds,
The dances and
bands,
soldiers and
baseball.
We discuss
So little on the
Factions and
Fights between the
Incarcerees and those
They called
Dogs
For turning inward to
Police their own
Or the
Resistance behind the
Riots and the bullets that
Hooked in to the
Runners who tried

To pass over barbed wire hurdles
Or
The old men losing
their minds and monthly earnings
in gambling circles from
one Block to the next
Or
The queer lovers, hiding
Or
The queer lovers, contributing
Or
The queer lovers, loving
Or
The girls, who
Screamed and winced,
Naked,
Outside
Of a thousand eyes
From the Stockade at Tule Lake.
We
Never
Speak much enough or at all
About
The
Fire.

N.T.N.C. – On Reparations, as guided by the legacy organizations, organizers, scholars, and other leaders of Black communities steering the movement to reckon with the harms of slavery, Jim Crow, and pervasive systems, policies, and institutions of racism that still thrive today.

Please –
Nikkei, JA family, please. When our Black community members (including our Black Nikkei folks) ask us to speak up for Redress and Reparations, say YES.

Stand up and say YES.

I know for some (or many) of you, that might not be your first reaction.

You might feel stress rise in your chest with an initial response that sounds like, "How on earth would that be possible? Who will pay for that? Slavery is in the past – how can we deal with it now?"

I will not shame you for your apprehension or skepticism. I instead invite you into dialogue. I will instead challenge you to place a solid pause on your hesitation or negation of the concept and the movement, and begin directing questions toward those leading the movement. They have been leading and building and researching and formulating and organizing the cause. For decades. Take in, first, the case for reparations as laid out by the many great minds doing the work. Allow yourself to reimagine life here for everyone as we finally move beyond this moment of reckoning, of uncovering the reality of racism and anti-Blackness and anti-Indigeneity that started in our foundations as a country and never ceased to dictate power and outcomes throughout every system since.

Give yourself permission to imagine real, feasible, actionable and concrete elevations in our institutions and systems. Imagine us a country being able to experience justice and peace that is so deep because, when it mattered, the people calling for it were listened to and their calls were heeded at (impossibly) long last.

As a person who wasn't incarcerated, but as a child and grandchild of those incarcerated at Manzanar and Tule Lake, I learned when I was a kid that there once was a time before camp reunions, and Pilgrimages, and monuments, and former American concentration camps gaining the designation of National Historic Sites. Let us always remember the government did not give us any of it – we had to go out and excavate our own memories. We had to find our history and fight for the revelation of our narratives. They meant to lock up the camps and all evidence and have us go on without acknowledging the pain of our existence. Without justice. Without healing. That was not possible. Our Sansei generation had to find out who they were in order to move forward. And they uncovered history. And they unlocked a reckoning.

We are not the moral authority on mass incarceration, mass removal, or collective infliction of oppression onto one community – we are linked to a larger cycle of struggle and also a legacy of resistance and solidarity. We have stood up to White Supremacy, time and again.

Let our lessons learned from Redress & Reparations for Japanese Americans serve to remind us that we were once told it was impossible, that it would never happen, that it was part of what happens at a time of war, or that the camps were not even that bad or it was necessary and good for us.

Let us remember that the strength and leadership came from within and had the solidarity of countless other people and communities in order for justice to come to fruition.

Let us remember that we also had strife and differences of opinion within the community, but we also knew we needed to trust ourselves and be trusted to figure it out for ourselves.

Let us remember we demanded the respect of being able to lead our own movement.

When we are asked to stand up and speak out in support of Reparations, I dare you to have your first answer be a standing YES. We will learn and converse and figure out the rest together, as guided by those in the Black community leading the movement. Let's start from YES and how do we support this, see this through, do our part to help make this happen?

Let us not only support Reparations because we once won a battle for Redress. Let us do it because it is the right thing to do, because it is an imperative toward healing for all, because we are being called upon, because in our deepest core – we know we must say YES in order for the healing of all.

Let us remember we will never truly breathe whole breaths, as whole beings, as a whole country and people, until we reach a collective reckoning, and repair...until we become whole and so can exhale into a place of healing at the depths of the blood and marrow in our bones.

Imagine that breath.

I say all of this here as plainly and directly as possible to you now because I love you. I believe in us. I believe we are a part of a much bigger We. And we are in the position now to fight for and alongside more of Us. Because we are facing the open gashes of our humanity. Because we must do this for us – all of us.

N.T.N.C. – on the Grandmas, the Comfort Women

Sometimes I can't believe how scary it feels to bring this up with so many of you.

Sometimes I can't fathom how long we have been arguing about this.

I once went toe-to-toe with The Horse's Mouth in the Rafu Shimpo regarding his denial of the Comfort Women. The radicals supported me and voiced further their own editorials, while I received a few finger-shakes in my face by conservatives at community events. And this was over 15 years ago.

For those of you in the community still saying "the Japanese government has apologized" – I must request...I must challenge that you watch the first 5 minutes of SHUSENJO, a film by Miki Dezaki. The kernel and the whole truth is right there. You can witness a Grandma. Grandma Lee Yong-soo. It centers on her truth.
You can see her heart is ripped apart – it comes through in the way she is screaming at a Japanese official who cannot look her in the eye.
She is not done fighting.
She is not at peace.
Watch that and put yourself in the same room with her.
And contemplate this: However the Japanese government tries to deny the history of Comfort Women or explain the ways they have apologized does not matter. It is for the survivor to say whether they have been answered and healed. It is for their children, grandchildren, and descendants to say. There, in their blood and bones is where we must go to listen and take heed. Their memories are louder than decades worth of denial and hollow apology.

To bring this up challenges us to consider the power in some
of our most revered institutions, and I do wonder who will
turn their backs on these words. But I no more lose breath
at this thought than I do at the calls we hear of the
Grandmas from all over the world, present and past.
Do you see? We are standing in the face of open wounds.

I want to know – what do you think comes next?

an homage for Yuri...

(delivered at the Los Angeles Memorial for Yuri
Kochiyama on August 31, 2014)

You were

the first stamp on the letter for the least likely to
receive
the last one to forget a face
first finger at the light switch
the last one to leave

countless many hold their
"first time I met Yuri"
story
as if it happened yesterday

before meeting her
i didn't understand
the meaning
of *Star Struck*
until
my bones shook and
the skin on my arms shrieked
the moment she walked in
from a sweltering J-Town afternoon
to rest at Alison's desk

i was 20 years old
an intern for Karen at the museum
trying to swallow my gasp
the first time i saw her face

"YOU'RE YURI!"
my excitement couldn't help itself
my brain, taking snapshots, shifted
my eyes toward her hands, her little legs,
finally fixating on her teeth

until
she did what i came to learn
she did for everybody
she broke out her notebook
she wrote down my name, my hometown, and my school
she asked which camps my parents were in
she mentioned all the people i should meet
she forgot she had come inside to rest

she was a conversation in pendulum form
a swift switch with steadfast passion
from politics to grandchildren

she made me lose track of the clock
the temperature
and even the fact that i had been
trying to memorize her face

she let me see an awesomely regular lady

i watched her become ordinary
in
the
most
extraordinary way

You were

>the rebel with a mission
the perpetrator of Talk The Talk, Walk The Walk
the surprise on the other side of the bull horn
the nation's most dangerous in disguise

when someone doesn't recognize
her name
i find myself telling them

of the Japanese American woman
in cat's eye glasses
pictured next to Malcolm X
in his final moments

i say she was an activist from Harlem to Redress
a mentor to the Asian American Movement
an advocate alongside political prisoners
i mention her
Nobel Peace Prize nomination
i quote the Blue Scholars:
"When I Grow Up, I Wanna Be Just Like Yuri Kochiyama"

but those are just my lead-ins
what people really get is
when i say she
was equal parts water and fire
speech so fluid

that the same love flowed in her cries
to Free Mumia
as
it did to surface in gratitude for those

who added to her beloved teddy bear collection

And on the day she died
i combed through every news channel
for a glimpse of her

Public radio and internet got it right

But the passing of a Revolution was not televised

i felt sorry only for the news stories
They missed out on but one cycle of our
Extraordinary Yuri

You are

   water hose to the crooked warden
   flood light to the invisible prison
   earthquake underneath the gatekeepers' feet

i imagine Yuri
sitting at a chair nearest the front door
leaning forward to tie her shoes
notebook and pen
in the fanny pack
already secured around her waist
checking off yesterday's list in her head
tabs spilling off the sides of today's schedule

i think of the times
she sat on panels and
we saw her eyebrows get twisted
at the question

by activists decades her junior
on the issue of burnout

i heard her say in one way or another
that there is so much to do
there isn't time left
to
think of herself
getting tired

i imagine Yuri again
and
see
humility
excusing itself
and
revolution reflecting on
its future

i see
no wasted motion
a kind of Zen
without the stink of religion

i see
no rest for her weariness
no ego to prove

For a collection of her selected speeches
students at UCLA were keen
to include her handwritten notes
for a talk she gave on Malcolm X
to students in the 2nd and 3rd grade

In it, she shared an autograph
Malcolm wrote
to her daughter:

"*Audee. Please help to
make this a better
world for all people.*"

"*This is probably the
message he would give
to you – if he were here
today.
And he is here in
spirit.*

'*To live in hearts that
are left behind is not to
die.*'
*Remember that – should
you ever lose someone
dear to you...*

*We, who loved Malcolm,
keep him alive in our
hearts.*"

Yuri

who
tossed the cells of the ivory tower
in
open-ended questions

iron-clad ideals
and principles that didn't flinch

You are

> happiness in the pursuit of freedom
> justice at the hands of peace
>
> the way the walk sprints
> the way the talk chants in the streets
> the way social justice dresses itself every morning
> the way self-determination decides to breathe
> the all ways affirmative action
> visitation that refuses to leave
> the metal cup clanging across the prison bars
> harbinger to the fire alarm
> theory in motion
> articulation in practice
> hammer to clock
> blowtorch to burnout
> bridge to the bridges

i quote from You in honor of You

Yuri,

You are the fire
who reminds us
to
make this a
better world
for all people

This is the message
we would give to you
if you were here today
and
You are here in
spirit

To live in hearts that
are left behind is not to
die

Remember, now that we have lost a giant

We, who love you, honor you,
keep you alive in our hearts
forever
in every single
extraordinary
and
ordinary
way

N.T.S.

8 billion alive. Well over 100 billion dead. Where did all
that ash and skin and blood and bone and energy go if not to
hang out and potluck once in a while with the energy of the
trillions more deceased animals and plants? That might
actually be very terrible. There could be an incredible
amount of universal lamentation circulating throughout our
systems.

Perhaps climate change is a combination of human ravaging of earth's resources and the mourning of our actions by the dead. Or maybe it is an offering – An energetic cosmic system of 100 million orchestras trying to enjoy their own nirvana, coming together for a final gift of generosity to Earthlings: a set of warnings via natural disaster in hopes that we finally learn to treat self, other and all, through every waking moment, as if the flood was rising and the fire was down the block, and we had no other thought but to call out, grab the first hand, look for every last person, ask for help, make sure everyone was okay. How will you do more of this in your every day, from week to week, month to month, season to season? What introductions do you need to make with your neighbors? Where are the unnatural disasters that need more of our attention and what are you going to do next?

Life is quickly disappearing. Have something good to report when you join the Dead.

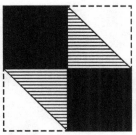

Do Not Attempt
Landing

Death Moment – 16

three juniors playing five seniors in chicken on Sepulveda.
we were off to rent *Three Men & A Baby* at The
Warehouse. Then. hit,
boom, sail, sail, float, blink, void, hush, no flash of life, just the
nothing silence.

middle back seat of would-be vinyl cemetery in an Accord
before center belts, sandwiched between Cathy and Yoko, all
the glass, in our skin.
surpassed near-death, i said *okay* to Dead, nodded head,
okay. Then. jaws-of-
life came to pull me out of proportion, lights back up, boom, the
everything noise.

bury the half-truth joke of coincidence, (not much) before
dying. that. day.
bury: the old self; the nothing to lose before now; the fascination
with a friend who took theirs – we had been standing near a
sidewalk, staring at our feet on grass, on asphalt, talking about
cousins and futures, then nothing of him – death, alive, gone,
too soon
bury *can't/ shouldn't/ don't/ maybe/ okay if
dead*...alive.now.every.thing.Promise: forget never living.

N.T.S.

        hide (this)

               for
               now.

N.T.S.

               tell her
               (not)
               to
               read
                    this
                    part.

N.T.S.

      forgive
          your
             self

          for
          how long
             this
               has taken
               to
             get
        out.

N.T.S.

forgive

your

self

for putting some

stories

back

into

the earth.

promise to

forgive

your

self

again when

you

dig

them

up

later.

N.T.S.

remember:

some

stories

are

for

the living.

other

                    stories are for
                                          some
                                time
                    long after
they

                                          have
                                          moved on
                                from
        this place.

        N.T.S.

        the
        balance:

                                somewhere
                                between
                                revealing
                                only what
                                she can handle
                                with
                                what your
                                bones
                                can
                                no longer
                                carry

                                [where does her story
                                               end
                                and mine begin to
                                        unravel?]

N.T.M.

Thank you (in advance)
For the
Permission.

(untitled)

.

.

.

a rope

a plastic bag

a bottle of pills

there are words
a mother should
never say to her
daughter
no matter how
accustomed they've
grown to the benefits
of honesty
between them

the right time to do it

tying the loose ends

or perhaps
they are exactly
the words
that need to be said
and planted
and kneaded
and stretched
and drilled
and hammered

and sewn
and drawn
and painted
and glued
and sealed
and peeled
and tried on
again and again
and worn
twice, thrice,
umpteen times over
and busted
and ripped
at every seam
until everyone
comes undone
and the words
come undone
and they become
just words
and

exhaust pipe

means

nothing

not
a thing
not one goddamn thing
worth
doing anything with

except
to remember to
forget
they have
any use
whatsoever at all

.

.

.

Stats:

"Among females from all racial backgrounds between the ages of 65 and 84, Asian Americans had the highest suicide rate." [1] [2]

"Asian Americans are less likely to seek professional help for psychological distress and they are less likely to self-disclose suicidal thoughts without the clinician's prodding." [3]

N.T.S.

This one feels too real.
But you need to show it to her anyway.
She will see she's not alone.
And I'd like to think that,
because she hates doing what everyone else does,
she'll ditch the ideation, for good.

1   Heron, M. (2011). Deaths: Leading causes for 2007. *National Vital Statistics Reports, 59, 8.*

2   Xu, J., Kochanek, K.D. Murphy, D.L., & Tejada-Vera, B. (2010). Deaths: Final data for 2007. *National Vital Statistics Reports, 58, 10.*

3   Ka Yan Cheng, J., Fancher, T.L., Ratanasen, F., Conner, K.R., Duberstein, P.R., Sue, S., and Takeuchi, D. (2010). Lifetime Suicidal Ideation and Suicide Attempts in Asian Americans. *Asian Am J Psychol, 2010 Mar.*

N.T.S.

I am a little crazy.
This is very normal.

N.T.M.

We are the ones
who are left.
You are all that
matters now.
Sometimes
we have to
tell ourselves:
Forget the
Dead.

For the Friend Who Says They Don't Feel the Need to Ask for Help or Get Therapy

It is not a matter of
Feeling

When it comes
I don't
Feel

Depression

I become a set of desires:

to
succumb to
the 8 LB.
weights under my eyes on my
temples inside my
throat resting in
my chest

to
finish something
Big
and have
the excuse to
run away forever

to
run so fast I
will have my spine stripped
away from my body's center
because I am

situated away from
my body's center

I
become an assortment
of singular elements
lying on my bed, loosely
strung together:

I am
suffocation

I am a length of
rope

I am
denial

I am a
spiral facing downward

it is not a
Feeling

I am these things
until I am not these things

until I
have dug up
the set of tools
I have used before
to dig me out
and
have employed

them sufficiently
barely
enough
so my body can grab at some air
and my ribs draw each other close
and my past relinquishes an inhale
and I can hear the words from
Dr. Joan when she was still alive
telling me
the strategies I used as a child
were for survival
but can become tethers as
an adult
and what is simple is not
always easy and
sometimes I need to start
with focus on a single
breath
and a gasp
emerges
and I use the rope I once was
to pull me out
and
gently lasso
bits of air
to become
the sum of
a splintered self grasping onto
whole parts of
process and risk and doubt and forgiveness and writing and
painting and breathing and counseling
yes so many years of counseling
and gratitude
for the lessons from a
dead therapist

until
I am a person who can stand
and
leave this room
for a nice while
or for
however long
I can
feel
what I am

N.T.S.

Remember to nurture and utilize your tools:

(breathe long breaths, imagine
the number of stones increasing in your palm, breathe)
(write, write, write)
(walk fast, jog, run)
(process with Joycey)
(employ the lessons from Dr. M) (simple, but not easy)
(take a 5 and walk outside)
(Reiki and Sekhem-Krem with Jaclyn)
(write, breathe, write, paint, write, breathe)
(hit the bag)
(take a nap with Brownie)
(have a conversation with the Dead – Dad, Bachan, Grandpa,
John, Wakako, Dean, Karen, Daryl, Arnold,
thank you for listening.)
(with Ma, learn an old dish, whittle together, ask questions)
(morning constitutional with Ollie)
(reach out to a Big Sis)
(drive)
(drive and sing)
(hear Nobuko's voice: Bambutsu – a thousand things all
connected)
(meditate on Gratitude)
(drive, and have a conversation out loud with yourself)
(drive and head write)
(call Kathy)
(drive, pull over, write)
(process with a living person other than yourself)
(dance alone, dance to a video, take a dance class)
(process with someone much older than yourself)
(sand some wood, burn it)
(carry Honey Cat around the house)

(breathe, yoga with Shin & Keiko, breathe)
(meditate on various routes towards forgiveness)
(process with someone much younger than yourself)
(read five books at once – fill up)
(create a space with other artists – fill up)
(attend a play, an event, a meeting – fill up)
(create something, anything – release)
(Trust The Process)
(stop going to so many meetings)
(Be Available To Yourself)

Undo. Unlearn. Unleash.
Unlessen. Unlasso. Unshrink.
Uncover. Unsmall. Unbridle.
Unbeneath. Unbecome. Unfasten.
Unarm. Ungrab. Unease.
Unlock. Unpress. Unstarfuck.
Unborder. Unboundary. Unswallow.
Unearth. Unshadow. Unhide.
Unhinge. Unwind. Unchain.
Uncringe. Unshoulder. Unsuperwoman.
Untether. Unguilt. Unmartyr.
Unpass. Unbreak. Unmold.
Unwar. Unbomb. Unbattle.
Untake. Unflagellate. Unsuccumb.
Unsubmit. Unbow. Unnod.
Unwall. Unhate. Unpost.
Uncoin. Undominate. Unstop.
Unwaver. Unbind. Unjudge.
Unshoot. Unload. Unshirk.
Unbury.

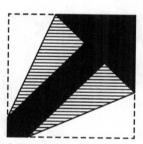

**O K to Land—Arrow
Shows Landing Direction**

To Fukaya Michiyo

(after riKu, who introduced me to Michiyo; after
Michiyo Fukaya; after Mikiso Hane)

"We are the daughters
Of the sea, moon and sun."
      – Michiyo Fukaya

A dream
shook me awake too soon.

We sat in a circle of fire
formed by your fingernails
to surround us in the Meiji era of
womxn shouting:
Kusunose Kita
wielding tongue of suffrage, of
anarchist, iconoclast:
Kanno Sugako, Kaneko Fumiko
weaving through the flames with us, they
urging us toward revolution, faced you
coaxing them from the men who drove them away, me
collecting my desire in the path of your ashes.

i woke to your words at my bedside:

        There is no way out
        Except madness or death

and
see the cracks, mirror reflections
of our mothers
in the pinch of yesterday's light.

We share:
the
same

wrong dirty name,

ease with
confrontation,

hunger for the
luscious food.

i have searched
endlessly, dire histories of
our ancestors to
find what earns your spirit.

i open
every body, looking
for your tongue.

i suspend myself
in your life's tether, cut
from the same cloth, your
sanity's nomenclature, your
rebel being,
loving and cursing
the verses that link
us.

We search all our lives
For beauty   *there,*

is your ember.

My mere pledge:

Take every chance to burn old
self,
Ignite every fire
inside,
Evoke you, the inferno

     Who will always be with me.

N.T.PartnersInGeneral (except for the RJ)

free / lone some highway

let me alone,
to roam, to run,
to be near you,
when I want
to be near
you

body language

For every relationship – we get to place one star
somewhere on our bodies. I see you, and think, we
might be around the same age (or I started young
and you're just into constellation tattoos).

For every broken heart received – we get to trace the
shape, as skewed as we'd like, and decide where
it will show up on the formerly beloved's skin. I
kindly hid the mark of a black heart under their tongue.

For every broken heart given – we must place one
lump of coal in our throats. It will show up as
a bulky Adam's Apple, without the perks of any
better vocal quality when speaking or singing.

It is only there to remind us, when that person shows
up in the future, why we should miss them and that they
are beautiful. When that time most surely comes, we
won't be allowed to say a thing, only swallow the moment.

The justice of heartbreak – we are all left with marks.

a brief essay leading up to The Anne Heche Reference

A friend once said,
"That's right. You're still Queer."
and I burst out laughing, which startled her and made the
words she spoke float up and hover right there in front of
her eyes.

So I explained that I usually just call myself
Queer
without using the word
Still
and from my tone she knew we could smile it off and leave
the thought in the air between us
without launching into a history lesson of my relationships.

Terminology is a funny thing and I know it gets complicat-
ed when people saw me with a cis man while watching the
word
Queer
make its way into my introduction at meetings or whenever
it just comes up because it can and, well, it does

Before I stumbled upon the identity of
Pansexual
I at times gave up and proffered the word
Bisexual
especially to the curious uncle or auntie, only to get the
ubiquitous, "Ohh, I see...I think." Even then, some would
say,"But...you're with...him." My gut reaction was to ask
if they'd only ever been with one person their entire life -
maybe thus the confusion?
Instead I'd end up

divulging either my sexual resume or a blank stare, both
saying far too much.

The second time I told my mom I love all kinds of bodies
was the first time she heard me because now, the Other body
in the relationship waiting for me at home made my feelings
Official
in her book.
I understood, it's complicated.
I reminded her I'd already come
out
to her before, in my early 20s.
Mom didn't flinch really, didn't even miss a beat.
She asked me,

"Is this an Anne Heche thing?"

My eyebrows did their usual What The Hell thing.

"No men before Ellen.
Like a phase kind of thing?"

I contemplated this for a while, feeling delighted, that the
very first
verbalized reaction from Mom had a touch of pop culture
savvy to it.
I didn't even know she knew about Ellen and Anne Heche.
I didn't want to forget the moment.
And I didn't want either of us to mess it up with more use-
less
language. I just sat there smiling...mouthing and repeating her
words.
sometimes moms can say the funniest things
in the very best moments.

the glory of religion (we understand why they can't come out)

(for m and q)

they colonized her homeland
with a familiar creed and spoke
on behalf of their god
and lied through
their teeth
about
Love

so she raised you to believe
you will kill her if
one day you pry
open your chest
and show her
who chews
at your
heart

N.T.A.O.U.Q.
I once heard an ally-uncle say his fantasy
is to host a big hall full of families, wholly
present to witness the coming out of their
child and that child and an other's child

and just one after the other after the other,
like a room of folks testifying and receiving
witness and just a whole bunch of queers
coming out in front of every single person
in their family. Said our community would
be healed once this happens.

Ally-uncle, maybe that is not for you to say.
Coming Out isn't always the only way to
happiness. There are queers with extremely
full lives full of love and family – chosen and
otherwise – and a way of living and being that
is healthy and not out in a way that is obvious
or verbalized. Please let each Queer friend
of yours decide for themselves the way they
want to be at any given moment with any
given family member, blood or not. And
don't be surprised if they tell you they are
healthy, satisfied, joyous, whole.

Where we would have gone

and then there were those who said
it was best I didn't come out to you
before you died
your generation, being the rusty
sunken treasure chest
that it is, or so they'd say

but I insist on my ability to predict the past:

it would have happened in July,
your dying wish that final year
you knew wasn't yours

a trip with all the grandkids,
aunties, uncles, cousins,
calabash and by blood

all aboard the biggest ship for the cheapest price,
a floating island of humans, midsummer,
the worst combination for sanity

I would have waived my right to a vote,
packed my trepidations and
prepared an entirely new way of breathing

all eyes would be on the space
between you and my girlfriend, but despite all assumptions,
you would be just fine

/ because the summer before / sitting down for lunch that
should have been hamburgers
or tacos or anything you wanted / me, hunched underneath

another failed relation-
ship / the warning of others i'd made the wrong choice / again /
there / i was / trying to
defend / promise / i will / be fine / i promise / i know what i'm
doing / all you knew
was to / leap / from your chair / forget the pockmarked liver /
tethering you to your
seat / put your hand on my shoulder / make everyone else turn
to vapor / say / one thing / to me:

you okay, kid? I just want you to be okay. /

and it would happen on the deck of a ship
at the end of two behemoth weeks

enough time for you to witness Joycey being to you
the way she is with the rest of the world

i would pretend never to catch you catching this
and come the sunset of our trip
after wave upon wave of sticky toddlers, sopping wet miniature
cargo shorts
stomping alongside sloppy drunk men-children,
expertise gained of every open bar available before 3:00pm
and the mastering of overwhelm by every buffet

the better part of me slumped in my designated chaise lounge
barely the gumption to lift my neck in time to see you

standing at the edge of the deck, pressing your midsection
against the rail, pretending you didn't need painkillers

Joycey would walk over,
ask:

How you doin' George

you would put your hand on her shoulder

I'm okay, kid. I'm doin' okay.

and there would never be a better thing said,
never a better time had

if i never meet your father

we will have surpassed our own
expectations

i already learned to love a man who
may never want
to know me

who never asks
what driveway
his daughter calls home
what past you have
untethered
what people call you
family

when you see me hunkered down
over my journal
you half joke and ask
if i'm writing a poem about you

i will say
this

we
managed to define
romance:

as in
triumph,
  as in knowing the greatest
  feat wasn't coming out,
  it was leaving,
  together,
  intact,

as in
peace

**Indicate Direction of
Nearest Civilization**

On America, Election Eve

(after Joshua Bennett; after Rocío Carlos)

We were stuck on the 110 freeway traveling south
Out of nowhere my mother tells me she was my age
when she realized why she's been angry all these years
Always in Los Angeles those deep conversations while driving
avoiding eye contact while staring into history's abyss
She'd
read an article in the LA Times on childhood experiences
and their lasting effect on the adult psyche
No sooner did she say aloud *Of course, that's a no-brainer,*
then did the room begin to spin, newsprint leaping off the page
turning like her stomach, from black to blue to white to red,
Flooding
her mind with the times her temper flared at lunches with
neighborhood ladies who filled her belly with their discomfort
Said she was *Too Angry* and too often *Talking About Race*
Said *Things Weren't That Bad*
and *There She Goes Again*
And
futile chats turned into argument
turning their chins in all directions away from her
Leaving her alone to stare at paper plates of
potato salad and potluck disdain
in a room full with the chatter of deafening silence
That
article was penned in the 1980's when I was called
like she'd been called as a child in the 40's:
Japs Go Home
I hadn't known the auto industry was crumbling
on the other side of our country

But
neither had any of the kids at school, or the ones
near the mall with their bikes and breezy threats, or
the ones in between aisles of cassette singles at
the record store, always whizzing by
with the same combination of words everywhere I went
I
was convinced they were from the same church or
underground after school club, given
a secret dictionary of terms and tactics
to show kids like me what colors we were to use
within the lines they draw around us

I
came to learn then of the *Sundown Towns*
my neighborhood, a brand of its own kind – where
Black and Brown folks get pulled over suddenly
and the cars that speed past have
Buy American bumper stickers all over the back
I
was learning
I was learning
I was learning the
different versions of
America
The
version that had my mother face those lunching ladies, but
instead see FDR, see barbs stuck in tumbleweed, see her
color
fade from America's mirror, see her father, so broken that
sometimes the vapors of sake and whiskey
were the only words his body could speak

I
imagine with hope how she might have finally seen herself, a
full grown adult when Grandpa revealed his deepest
moment of pride in the time she was 2 ½ years old,
a miniature hurricane in dusty shoes,
instructing the rest of the family they were not to
leave
for Grandma's just because the Army had set
up shop on their farmland for the war effort, scaring
her older brother to tears, those soldiers positioned next
to the Kato Nursery sign, their rifles taking root in the
soil

This is our
Home
She screamed
This
Is our home

My mother's anger formed my bones
to flow through my blood and
stand ready at the back of my throat
Her voice, a generational echo chamber
for the whispers who came before her
Each
one of the past, giving permission
or perhaps begging
those who come next
to be louder than the last
She
is in her eighties now, has learned
to transfer less ire
onto the women of her earlier years
She'd found a much bigger enemy
in yet another president

She
curses his name while
writing Get Out The Vote postcards
to our neighbors in Arizona and
Florida with great fury and
cursive that looks like flowers yelling
I
wonder if she ever gives her anger
credit for the compassion
that spews
out of her mouth, like
a few years prior, half
conscious
and losing blood after routine surgery,
using what little energy she had
to lament for those
without healthcare and
to continue cursing the president
She
is not only my link to our family's trauma
but is the courage unlocked from deep
inside our ancestral sinew
Carries all the reasons for my reasons,
The heat in my blood
These
hands that knew to break the
flesh-colored crayon in half and move on
These lungs that helped me yell at that white man
for cheating against me in a child's game at
Circus Circus when I was 4 years old
These
feet that leapt up from my desk
to disrupt our 11th grade Government class
arms outstretched to the teacher *too often* with
articles our textbooks refused to teach

My
mother's mouth that lives through
this mouth
so full of fire there is little room
left for air and I
can not keep it shut
And

when it is time for her to look back for
the last time I will be there to remind her
the best of her fire remains the
strongest of my colors and I thank the
universe and all versions of heaven
that her anger is
Evergreen

Letters to Taz, Summer 2020

Dear Taz,

I dare wonder where this finds you.

I read the text on
the latest about your health,
and came to my desk, head bowed in
acknowledgment – our letters
have become tiny flags we use
to pin a map
with the trials
we face
across generations
and time

in this place we carve
poetics of penpalship, conjure
spaces for our ghosts to meet and
drink and pray and exchange
laughter and hauntings

but I didn't want to convene
ever
in this new fashion that binds us now,
the presence of illness or
questions on diagnosis
and second opinions on second opinions –
what did the doctor say is next?
Always now: What is next?

I did not wish
to gather around

the biopsies to your schedule or the
unspoken decisions of an arcane womb

but our paths come to this
regardless of resistance
or anticipation
we are pieces
of an energetic telegram
sent back and forth over the ages
our bodies are not ours alone

for cancer scares to cancer cells
they are all alarms
a call to find ourselves at some unwanted
unclean slate we must wipe long enough
to find the silver lining

and our poems are bloodlettings
and my letters are part question, part prayer,
even to a Muslim from an Agnostic

and, all ways,
my words here sound like wishes
but I promise are pledges to you –

that our next exchange will
be in reminiscence
of the writing retreat of our dreams
in Joshua Tree or Lake Arrowhead, some
long expanse of respite and productivity

I will write no sooner
than in celebration of
a time
where I finally heed your request

to draw up your well, get
you to
breathe in so deep,
crack so wide open and sob
the long and aching cry your ancestors
have been waiting to hear

I will write no sooner than
in recognition
of the corner you turned in your body
and you will return
in the same manner to me –

when we reclaim the bones. and embrace the DNA. and
strip the marrow of any visible layers of solitude. and
extract the tender secrets who've been waiting to be
discovered. and shake the ground underneath future's tether
to our illnesses. and gather around the greatest fire with all
of our cousins, past and future, all present, all aglow,

and we will speak solely
wholeheartedly
eternally
from that moment,

of healing.

love,
me

But my favorite moment during cancer...

Nurse wheels me out of prep. Whizzing past the waiting room. On the way to my lumpectomy. Wait. Stop. Out of the corner of my eye. Mom. Where she was supposed to be. In the waiting room. But now in her own wheelchair. With her own nurse standing next to her.

What's going on, Ma?

> *Oh, I don't know.*
> *I just started feeling really bad.*
> *I almost fainted.*

Oh. Kay.
Well. Take it easy.
Did you drink some water?

> Nurse says:
> She has high blood pressure.
> Don't worry, Mama.
> It's just anxiety.

> (Mom looks genuinely confused.)

> *Anxiety?*

> *This is embarrassing.*
> *This is supposed to be about you.*
> *You're the one going into surgery.*

> (her voice wavers through that last word.)

(posture stiffens.)
(big exhale.)

But,
It's not ANXIETY.
I mean,
I don't know why I'd be anxious.

Me and my nurse   and mom's nurse   share a look.

(Oh, no reason, right?
It's just your kid, with a tube connected by two needles
wired through the breast, held together by a plastic cup and
surgical tape, on their way to an operation at the beginning
of our road to beat down a tumor after weeks of battling to
get better medical insurance.)

Ma. It's okay.
I
          Am

               Having

                    S U R G E R Y.

                                   For

                                             CANCER.

And then I burst.

Laughter.

My left boob quivers and yelps when I move

under all the surgical paraphernalia.
But I can't stop.

We both get wheeled into the same elevator.
Ma finally joins us, now a choir of cackles.
Two generations in wheelchairs,
ascending past worries and what-ifs.

I take a selfie.
I want to remember the laughter.

Grandpa was, like, radical

Me. middle school aged. Staring at a photograph of
my grandfather.
A panorama of the farmers
at Manzanar.

Staring til my feet started to
tingle from
planting myself like a rude
patron in the middle of
that museum in Independence.

Trying to figure it out.

He had a long, black
beard.

Like no one else in that
photograph.
Like no other photos I'd seen
of him,
before or after the war.

Fast forward several years and twenty years
after his death.

Annual new years lunch and
Uncle Tommy, always with the best stories about Grandpa.

Grandpa as usher across the
border, sneaking in friends
from Kaseda into California,

Grandpa and his brother,
fighting drinking fighting,
Kagoshima always in their
blood and at the tops
of their lungs.

But what about that   beard?

Simple,
Tommy said.

Protest.   Your   *Grandpa said he*
                                  didn't need to be
                                  pretty in camp.

Said he'd keep his   *beard*
                                  as long as they
                                  were keeping him.

Those words rooted in me
like the
hands of a cosmic god
reaching into a dormant
patch of history had pulled
me up, flung
me loose.

struck me
like the world's largest choir
breaking into song alongside
a 1500-foot organ and
a 75-piece taiko orchestra.

like, I knew it all along,
fire in the blood is   genetic.

like I'd never need to
hear another story   on   Grandpa

                          ever   again.

unjaded

approach

      me   with an

          unfastened   mind

ready

    to be   ravished

               by

       the   entertainment

      of

  all

  absurd

      ideas   and   lashings

      upon

            institution

come   with   me

to

      lay

against the base
of willows

      and rediscover

the

truth

underneath
our
shadows

as   we

exchange questions with the abandon of fire

let
us   declare   an

a t t a c k

on   trademarked
labels

and   two-for-one
seminars

aimed

at the   weary

who   wish

nothing

more

than to be   told   an

answer

we

will   promise:
to feed
a path

of   simple

complexity,

agree   we are
surrounded

by   common

originality,

and   unfathomably understand   nothing
is as it
seems

l o v e
m e

with

an
unjaded

heart

and
a
soft soul

ready
to
be

taken
by none other
than

your   Self

and
in
that
trail
you
blaze
i

will

follow

N.T.W.

I wish you a Moment of Death. Is that too harsh to say or
too hard to hear? If only to have you come out of it fine
and ultimately unhurt – but to be shaken into life,
to be woken into the center of yourself, reaching first
for your own air, gasping at your own brilliance, granting
yourself the permission to say Yes to the initial whisper –
the one you fear to hold too long because it is the idea,
the challenge, the journey you know at the pit of your
intuition that you need to take. If only to go through some
end and exist in utter, undeniable gratitude, forgiveness,
and movement forward, to have you full of courage
and determination to weather by all means necessary
the overwhelming, ever-present, internal or external
force of fear.

N.T.R.

Write a list of your near-death experiences, what I
otherwise call Death Moments. Decide for yourself
what you term it. But you know what it is – even if for a
fraction of a second you imagined death in haste, in reality,
in a moment. Take this list and write into one of them.
What will you unbury? Contemplate this moment, along
with any others, that are the prime ingredients of a recipe
that make you who you are.

weeds

Let us grow peace
like a weed
that crawls up the sidewalks
of every street,
so pervasive, so profound,
it becomes
impossible to kill

Navigation Tips:

N.T.S. = Note(s) To Self

N.T.C. = Note To Community

N.T.W. = Note To World

N.T.R. = Note To Reader

N.T.N. = Note to Newcomer

N.T.M.G.Z.F. = Note To Millennial or Gen Z Friend

N.T.N.C. = Note To Nikkei Community

N.T.A.O.U.Q. = Note To Allies of Us Queers

N.T.A.A.A.C. = Note To Asian American Artists Community

N.T.M. = Note To Ma

Acknowledgments

Note to Self and Community and Universe
– in Acknowledgment, in Gratitude –
in gassho, as told to us by Reverend Mas Kodani –
acknowledgment of everything that happened in the
universe to bring us here, to this moment, right now.

N.T.S. – art+community, one word
+
N.T.S. – Solidarity is not transactional, charitable,
unidirectional and outward facing as in one doing for (an)
other…Solidarity is transformative work with self+other+the
world. Solidarity is a practice toward the elevation of all…
After –

The groundings, the light – Tuesday Night Project fam
circling the globe from back in 1998, including all staff
and volunteers and staunch supporters (past and present);
Vigilant Love fam, leadership, staff, steering committee
members; Nikkei for Civil Rights & Redress (NCRR); Nikkei
Progressives; Visual Communications; Great Leap and the
entire FandangObon family; the Okaeri Nikkei LGBTQ
Community; Comfort Women Action for Redress and
Education; Little Tokyo Service Center; our NP/NCRR joint
Reparations Cttee., the H.R. 40 Coalition, Legislative
Strategy Cttee., and Human Rights Watch.

The mapping, the fruition – this project affected that project
which affected this, to every single person who has touched
TALES OF CLAMOR, especially my partners in creative
crime, Kennedy Kabasares, NCRR, Howard Ho, Alison De
La Cruz, Dan Kwong, Nancy Keystone, the JACCC (Japanese
American Cultural & Community Center), Kinetic Theory

Circus Arts, V.C., our 2019 cast Kurt Kuniyoshi, Jully Lee, Sharon Omi, Greg Watanabe, and Takayo Fischer, and to the many collaborators over the years that most certainly informed and supported this work, including Kuniharu Yoshida, Akeime Mitterlehner, Ivy Chou, Eddy Vajarakitipongse, Peter Thornbury, Park Cofield, Network of Ensemble Theatres, New England Foundation for the Arts, Lynn and Brian Arthurs, and more than anyone, my Ma.

The playgrounds, the labs – Great Leap's Collaboratory; TeAdaWorks; DRAWN Residency, Toronto; Edge of The World, New York/Philly and all Asian Arts Initiative residencies, Philly; Asian Arts Freedom School, Toronto; Grand Park Teaching Writer residency; LTSC and the Japanese American National Museum for the +LAB Artists Residency; Pomona College AARC Artist Residency; Giant Robot, AP3CON and API Forward Movement (writing desk gratitude); Discover Nikkei; UCLA Aratani C.A.R.E.; Smithsonian APA Literary Festival; Kaya Press; Regent Press; UCLA Asian American Studies Center Press; International Women's Writing Guild; Deyan Audio; Penguin Random House Audio; Art Matters Foundation; and to the publications where a handful of the pieces in this book appeared in earlier forms: Heyday Books – Life After Manzanar; Bamboo Ridge Press – 40th Anniversary anthology; Chaparral Canyon Press – Open Doors; Tia Chucha Press – The Coiled Serpent; Temple University Press – Q&A Voices from Queer Asian North America; eohippus labs – Urgent Possibilities – Writing on Feminist Poetics & Emergent Pedagogies.

The embraces, the fire – To all those who made the time to review this work and write blurbs and offer up incredible support for its launchings ahead – from old friends to new colleagues, mentors – all heroes and forever teachers to the

many of us: Keiko Agena, Allan Aquino,
Xochitl-Julisa Bermejo, Sara Borjas, F. Douglas Brown,
Rocío Carlos, D'Lo, Ramy El-Etreby, Sesshu Foster, Dorothy
Randall Gray, Peter J. Harris, Narinda Heng, Naomi
Hirahara, Umi Hsu, Karen Ishizuka,
Dr. Ashaki Jackson, Naomi Ko, T.K. Le, Muriel Leung,
Sean Miura, Kate Maruyama, Kathy Masaoka, MILCK,
Daren Rikio Mooko, Sri Panchalam, Angela Peñaredondo,
Yumi Sakugawa, Faith Santilla, Zora Satchell, Beau Sia, Mike
Sonksen, Surrija, Dr. Curtiss Takada Rooks, Jenevieve Ting,
Terry Wolverton, Kristina Wong, Khaty Xiong, Jenny
Yang, and Mitsuye Yamada.

The origins – I wouldn't be in this moment without the first
book, *signaling*, and The Undeniables, and especially Erik
Matsunaga and Edren Sumagaysay.

The aircraft, the landing – And especially, to Writ Large
Press from their very beginnings through now – Chiwan
Choi, Judeth Oden Choi, Peter Woods, (and in those early
years, Jessica Ceballos Y Campbell) and now in concert with
The Accomplices (incl Janice Lee). This is because of all
of you and your vision, brilliance, patience, kindness, and
simply Chiwan's question back in 2012 – "What is your next
project? Can I publish it?"

N.T.S. – life lacks all luster without the constant inspiration
all around - the homies, the best friends, the truest true, the
longtime comrades, the mentors and teachers on all levels,
the ones who call just because, who invite me in to the lives
of your kids & furry babies, who I don't see enough but think
of always, who hold so much space for great conversation,
laughter, hard work, meals, dancing, learning, growing, joy
– the schools, the playgrounds and the chosen family I would
choose for every lifetime.
After –

Keiko, Shin Kawasaki, Kathy, Geneva Tien, Geri & Scott
Okamoto (thank you always for saving my life), Johneric
Concordia & Christine Araquel, Nobuko Miyamoto &
Tarabu Betserai Kirkland, Karen Ishizuka & Bob Nakamura,
Evelyn Yoshimura & Bruce Iwasaki, Patty & Steve
Nagano, Lynn & Brian, Kennedy, Daren, Naomi, Sean &
Andrew, Kathryn Bannai, Carrie Morita, Jan Tokumaru,
Kay Ochi, Suzy Katsuda, Janice Yen, Richard Katsuda, Jim
Matsuoka, George Abe, Jenny San Angel, Jason Fong,
Lauren Moon & Advait Thakur, traci ishigo & Eli Tizcareño,
Safiya & Sahar Pirzada & Imran Khan, Taz Ahmed, Liz
Kaufman, Mari Nakano, Simone & Claire & Dougi, Eka &
Skye & Emi & Mike, Rocío & Ana, Umi & Jacob, Professor
Glenn Omatsu, CSUF Asian American Studies Department,
Dr. Ellen Junn, Dr. Art Hansen, Dr. Craig Ihara, James To,
Sefa Aina, Ann-Margaret Webb, Tracy Nguyen-Chung &
Kiyoko Williams, Soomi Kim, Gertie Meza & Golda Inquito,
Tamlyn Tomita & Daniel Blinkoff, David Ono, Reed & Jack
& Ko & Kate, Mary Rose Go & Patrick Rosal, Amy
Uyematsu, Velina Hasu Houston, Eric Nakamura, Ed Lin
& Cindy Cheung, Rachel McLeod Kaminer, Lynell George,
Karineh Mahdessian, Jen Hofer, Natashia Deón, Kim
Ohanneson, Dana Vinke, Danny Thien Le, Clement
Hanami, Scott Oshima, Cindy Sangalang & Tad
Nakamura, Byron Dote & Alice Tong, Nanci & Anthony
Barrera, Mike Nailat & Lainey Dolalas, David Tran, Kai
Luen Liang, Alfie Ebojo, Vanessa Vela-Lovelace family, Kat
Carrido Bonds family, Quincy Surasmith, Sophie Wang,
Sophia Chang, Yazan, Mehak Anwar, Asiyah Ayubbi, Sarah
Jacobus, Connie Lim, Krista Suh, Jane Lui, Erin O'Brien &
Jeffy Middleton, Grace Umali, Mya Worrell, Alex Kanegawa
& Nara Kim, Kristin Fukushima, Joy Yamaguchi, Mark
Masaoka, Kimi Maru, June Hibino, Mike Murase, Mia
Barnett, Miyako Noguchi, Alan & Ruth Kondo, Zen
Sekizawa & Mario Correa, Eddie Wong, Susan Hayase &

Tom Izu, Linda Wei & Ashle Fauvre, Ryan Suda, Junko Goda & Daniel Park, Addie & Joanna Lee & Phil Yu, Philip Hirose, Sue Jin Kim, Sara & Aileen Omura & Glenn Suravech, Davina & Gayle Isa & Gary San Angel, James & Cindy Choi, Mitsuko Brooks, Miki Dezaki, Vickie Vertiz, Kenji Liu, Tammy Yamada, Eddy Gana Jr. and Steph Sajor, Jess X Snow, Kyoko Nakamaru, Ally Vega, Rino Kodama, Emmie Hsu, Skim, Sanusi, Audrey Kuo, Anu Yadav, Mari Ryono, Liz Sunwoo, Gein Wong, Angela Carlberg, Amber Trout, Sarah Parmenter, Nic Rademacher, Nikiko Masumoto, Katie Yamasaki, Imani Tolliver, Lisa Doi, Emily Akpan, Dreisen Heath, Kathy Yep, Deborah Wong, Stephen Sumida, Lucy Burns, Susan Kamei, Margo Okazawa-Rey, Martha Matsuoka, Sequoia Mercier, Kuida-Osumi family, Wong-Ito family, Christine & Erik Matsunaga family, and yet again, all the folks previously mentioned by full name, above.

N.T.S. – the life given to us now is surely fueled by the energy in our ether of the 100+ billion and countless numbers of animals & creatures who have passed through this planet's lifetime.
After - Dad, Bachan, Grandma, Grandpa, Kato and Kiriyama ancestors, Uncle Gene & Auntie Aiko, Uncle Jim, Ray Ochoa, Karen Gee, Miles Ono, Dean Matsubayashi, John Delloro, Darryl Daniels, Eddie Oshiro, Arnold Moreno, Karin Higa, William Hohri, Yosh Kuromiya, Frank Emi, Lloyd Inui, Sue Kunitomi Embrey, Linda Mabalot, Aiko Herzig-Yoshinaga, Wakako Yamauchi, Grace Lee Boggs, Yuri Kochiyama...

N.T.FamilyIncludingTheKids –
George, Willie, Miho, Bob, Judy, Bryce, Kyle, Cullen, Auntie Linda, and Kato and Kiriyama, Toya, Hasegawa, Endow, Sonoda, Tabata, Yamashita families, ancestors, and all of "The Kids" – I never see you enough but think of you

all, all the time. Thank you for your support from afar and for the everlasting memories I hold so close.

And to Norma, Liz, and Bobbi – thank you for sharing Joyce with me. Norma, let's please get your beautiful piano playing recorded – it's time. Liz, we are here for you. Bobbi, I love you and our magical times together!

N.T.the.RJF.
Raquel Joyce Fujimaki
Thank you for being everything you are – to me, your family, our furry babes, this world. Somehow I knew – but how could I have known, all those years ago at Shin's gig – that the colliding of our polar opposition would mean the 90% of our yin yang would be worth every percent it is not. You know I love you forever.

N.T.Mom.
I can't not write about you. You gave me life and everything I have. All of this is because of all of you. You have been my rock. It is an honor every time you let me be that for you.

...

[[For full Acknowledgments, Blurbs, Land Recognition, and Notes, please go to traciakemi.com]]

...

traci kato-kiriyama (they+she) – based on unceded Tongva, Gabrielino, Acjachemen, Kizh land – is an award-winning multi-, inter- and transdisciplinary artist, recognized for their work as a writer/performer, theatre deviser, cultural producer, and community organizer. As a storyteller and Artivist, tkk is grounded in collaborative process, collective self-determination, and art+community as intrinsically tied and a critical means toward connection and healing. She is a performer & principal writer for PULLproject Ensemble, two-time NET recipient; NEFA 2021 National Touring Project finalist for their show *TALES OF CLAMOR*. Their work is also featured in a wide swath of media and print publications (incl. NPR; PBS; Elle.com; *The Hollywood Reporter*; Entropy; Chaparral Canyon Press; Tia Chucha Press; Bamboo Ridge Press; Heyday Books; Regent Press). tkk is a core artist of Vigilant Love, member of the H.R. 40 Coalition, core organizer of the Nikkei Progressives & NCRR joint Reparations Committee, and Director/ Co-Founder of Tuesday Night Project (presenter of the Tea & Letter writing series and Tuesday Night Cafe space in Little Tokyo).

More Praise for *Navigating With(out) Instruments*

"traci kato-kiriyama's *Navigating With(out) Instruments* will expand your heart and spirit in all directions – in the marrow of your bones, deep into the earth, out into the streets, and into the stars and beyond where our collective radical imagination and our ancestors of past, present and future beckon us to listen more, ask more questions, stoke our hunger for justice, and love in ways that crack us open beyond what we believed possible." — **Yumi Sakugawa, author of** *Your Illustrated Guide to Becoming One with the Universe*

*

"*Navigating With(out) Instruments* is a remarkable undertaking. I am enamored with its breadth, its expanse, but mostly how it kept whispering questions in my ear: 'Did your grandma have a hearty laugh? Did your grandpa also like to drink? Where are the remains of their proudest echoes being stored?' Here kato-kiriyama lays out our necessary practice: keep your family present in the art you create; create art that celebrates community collaboration; keep your body linked to the body of work you will create. If we wrap ourselves with what she is telling us, if we do the dance *Navigating With(out) Instruments* invites us to do, then what ultimately happens is a glorious and continual flourishing." — **F. Douglas Brown, author of** *ICON*, **and** *Zero to Three*, **winner of 2013 Cave Canem Poetry Prize**

*

"traci kato-kiriyama is our time's flame bearer, warning us of past wrong turns, and shining light immediately in front of us. She belongs to the circle of poets who release words to restore, galvanize, and goad. I will be picking up *Navigating With(out) Instruments* often to remind myself where we've been and to determine where we need to go. An essential addition to a 21st century library." — **Naomi Hirahara, author of the *Mas Arai* series and *Clark and Division***

*

"A daring self exploration inviting us all to further honor what made us, cherish the breaths we share, and challenge the history that prevents our healing, our building, and our rise. It reminded me to expand my understanding of connection, gave me laughs that needed releasing, and affirmed the vulnerability I seek to be empowered by. Grateful for this needed addition to our shared story." — **Beau Sia, Tony Award winning poet (*Def Poetry*) and author of *Well Played***

*

"The elegy according to traci kato-kiriyama's *Navigating With(out) Instruments* is a hybrid lament in which grief shapeshifts time after time. Each loss that unfolds in these pages cracks open my heart, and I know immediately that only someone who has examined every indelible texture of this ache can write with such sharp clarity. I am put back together by the tenderness with which kato-kiriyama weaves in the love of and for a partner, family, community, and larger vision for social change in between deep mourning, inspiring a world in which we too can become 'impossible to kill.' This book has become my poetic guidepost for survival. May it be for you too." — **Muriel Leung, author of *Imagine Us, The Swarm* and *Bone Confetti***

*

"*Navigating With(out) Instruments* brings forth stories that tear me apart with the brutal beauty of the life blood that courses through traci and her ancestors. She invites me into her deeply feeling and perceptive spirit, building me back with more fire in my veins to continue striving for a life of true activism, art, love, and community. Her words made me feel my most sacred yearnings for a sense of belonging as an Asian American, a woman, and a human being who believes in the possibility for better. My heart sang and screamed with joy and catharsis, because reading her latest work is quenching my thirst to see a fellow Asian sister stand in all her sacred glory. The collection of poems and essays has left me feeling determined to dig deeper, to stand taller, and to walk the walk. This is truly an offering of traci's soul, and mine is richer after having read this. A must read." — **MILCK, songwriter and social change advocate behind** *Billboard*'s **#1 Protest Song of the Year (2017), the #icantkeepquiet movement, and The Somebody's Beloved Fund**

*

"The vivified words and remembrances forged here by artist traci kato-kiriyama offer that space inside the heart that remind us what a future breath might hold. 'A surprise,' 'a good memory,' or perhaps more simply, devastatingly, 'mercy for another time.' With striking aliveness and full-bellied meditations on death that surrender you—the reader—to traci, the liver, the survivor, the poet, the prayer. As if to say, here are the words that made me real. That made us die. That made us choose triumph, togetherness, and that 'wild dream' once more. Look at them, and memorize how they sing." — **Jenevieve Ting, Writer and Artist** "traci kato-kiriyama is one of my best friends. I feel I know her extremely well and yet this book brought me a whole new understanding of her. Intimate, profound, moving. It will grab your heart and tickle your mind. With intelligence and deep care, traci has delivered heartbreaking topics in a way that leaves you inspired and downright joyful. An absolute treasure." — **Keiko Agena, author of** *No Mistakes*; **"Lane Kim" on** *Gilmore Girls*

*

"traci kato-kiriyama's *Navigating With(out) Instruments* offers just the salve we need to soothe us in these difficult times. This collection reveals tkk to be an alchemist, who can take pain and grief, trauma and loss, and transform them into works of beauty. tkk dives deep and pours their bleeding heart into this collection, their truth and vulnerability lighting the way, bringing us along on their journey to healing, to wellness, to wholeness." — **Ramy El-Etreby, writer/performer (***The Ride***), applied theatre artist, storyteller, educator**

*

"*Navigating With(out) Instruments* is a set of captivating travels through life & death, discovery & recovery, while winding through country, ancestry, and identity. Never heavy handed, it connects by way of personal milliseconds magnified, exploded onto the page. Her words feel familiar and thoroughly compassionate, which makes this work spacious and patient – it made room for me to examine my own pile of stories at my own pace. And just as simply, it made me want to better enjoy my next breath. Anyone who knows traci would likely agree that these are profoundly true characteristics of what it feels like to have a conversation with her. In her true form, this work feels like that extended conversation over bottomless coffee. This work is built on steel beams of ancestry and blood memory, with rooms occupied by growing pains, birthday wishes, things unsaid, dancing, singing, who is owed, how we own. It is a beautiful guide on navigating toward our immeasurable capacity to live." — **Surrija, songwriter, recording artist, arranger, actor, and musician for Cambodian Rock Band, Off-Broadway**

*

"*Navigating With(out) Instruments* is a collection of regrets and what ifs; an accounting of the aftermath of option B when option A was the correct answer. It's an archive of a history that will never be recovered. But it's far more astute and thoughtful than a tale of the vulnerable underbelly of survival and struggle we all know exists and love to mythologize. traci's ability to be a curious student of her own personal tragedy and mourning – and have the nerve to write down her observations in the midst of it all – is a rare type of courage and intelligence that doesn't boast. Instead, it resonates. You could read *Navigating* in a couple of sittings, but I didn't. I put it down often to cry, but I also put it down to write. And I can't remember the last time a book of poetry ever compelled me to do both." — **Faith Santilla, Beatrock Music artist (*A Slow Build to Power*) and collaborator (Bambu - *Don't Send for the Others*; Ruby Ibarra - *Us*), poet, labor organizer**

"This book is a poetic murmuration of power and prompts that leaps towards the edge without fear of flight. traci's writings soar beyond definitions of storytelling and soliloquy with the mastery of a bard with no borders. Her words have given birth to a divine dominion that inculcates the insistence of truths laid bare, family as sanctuary, and memoir as a weapon of mass deconstruction. *Navigating With(out) Instruments*, a stellar creation of a word warrior and revolutionary auntie griot, is nothing short of superb." — **Dorothy Randall Gray, author of *Soul Between The Lines*, poet, artist, teacher, enchantivist**

***